The Metadata Manual

Chandos
Information Professional Series

Series Editor: Ruth Rikowski
(Email: Rikowskigr@aol.com)

Chandos' new series of books is aimed at the busy information professional. They have been specially commissioned to provide the reader with an authoritative view of current thinking. They are designed to provide easy-to-read and (most importantly) practical coverage of topics that are of interest to librarians and other information professionals. If you would like a full listing of current and forthcoming titles, please visit our website, www.chandospublishing.com, email wp@woodheadpublishing.com or telephone +44 (0) 1223 499140.

New authors: we are always pleased to receive ideas for new titles; if you would like to write a book for Chandos, please contact Dr Glyn Jones on gjones@chandospublishing.com or telephone +44 (0) 1993 848726.

Bulk orders: some organisations buy a number of copies of our books. If you are interested in doing this, we would be pleased to discuss a discount. Please email wp@woodheadpublishing.com or telephone +44 (0) 1223 499140.

Chandos Publishing
Hexagon House
Avenue 4
Station Lane
Witney
Oxford OX28 4BN
UK
Tel: +44(0) 1993 848726
Email: info@chandospublishing.com
www.chandospublishing.com
www.chandospublishingonline.com

Chandos Publishing is an imprint of Woodhead Publishing Limited

Woodhead Publishing Limited
80 High Street
Sawston
Cambridge CB22 3HJ
UK
Tel: +44(0) 1223 499140
Fax: +44(0) 1223 832819
www.woodheadpublishing.com

First published in 2013

ISBN: 978-1-84334-729-3 (print)
ISBN: 978-1-78063-395-4 (online)

British Library Cataloguing-in-Publication Data.
A catalogue record for this book is available from the British Library.

Typeset by RefineCatch Limited, Bungay, Suffolk

The Metadata Manual

A practical workbook

REBECCA L. LUBAS, AMY S. JACKSON AND
INGRID SCHNEIDER

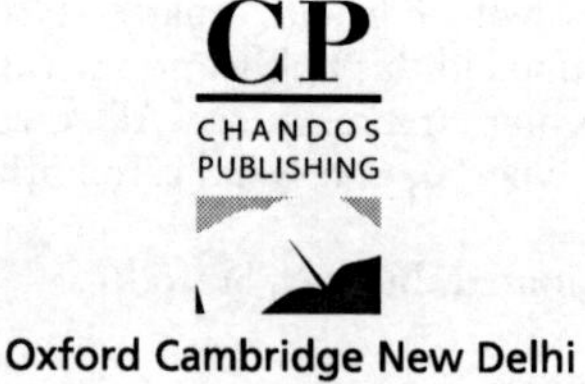

Oxford Cambridge New Delhi

Contents

List of figures and tables

Figures

Tables

List of abbreviations

AAAF	Anglo-American Authority Files
AACR	Anglo-American Cataloging Rules
AAT	Art & Architecture Thesaurus
AITF	Art Information Task Force
ARL	Association of Research Libraries
BHA	Bibliography of the History of Art
CCO	Cataloging Cultural Objects
CDWA	Categories for the Description of Works of Art
CONA	Cultural Objects Name Authority
DACS	Describing Archives: A Content Standard
DC	Dublin Core
DCMES	Dublin Core Metadata Element Set
DCMI	Dublin Core Metadata Initiative
DCMITYPE	DCMI Type Vocabulary
DHTML	Dynamic HyperText Markup Languages
DTD	Document Type Definition
EAD	Encoded Archival Description
FGDC	Federal Geographic Data Committee
FRBR	Functional Requirements for Bibliographic Records
HTML	HyperText Markup Language
HTTP	HyperText Transfer Protocol
ILS	Integrated Library System
ISAD(G)	General International Standard Archival Description
LC	Library of Congress
LCC	Library of Congress Classification
LCNAF	Library of Congress Name Authority File

LCSH	Library of Congress Subject Headings
MARC	MAchine-Readable Cataloging
MLA	Modern Language Association
MODS	Metadata Object Descripton Schema
NCSA	National Center for Supercomputing Applications
NISO	National Information Standards Organization
OAC	Online Archive of California
OAI	Open Archives Initiative
OAI-PMH	Open Archives Initiative Protocol for Metadata Harvesting
OCLC	Online Computer Library Center
OWL	Web Ontology Language
RDA	Resource Description and Access
RDF	Resource Description Framework
SES	Syntax Encoding Schemes
SGML	Standard Generalized Markup Language
TARO	Texas Archival Resources Online
TEI	Text Encoding Initiative
TGM	Library of Congress Thesaurus for Graphic Materials
TGN	Thesaurus of Geographic Names
ULAN	Getty Union List of Artist Names
URI	Uniform Resource Identifier
VRA	Visual Resources Association
W3C	World Wide Web Consortium
XHTML	eXtensible HyperText Markup Language
XML	eXtensible Markup Language
XSD	XML Schema Document
XSLT	eXtensible Stylesheet Language Transformation

Acknowledgements

We would like to thank a number of individuals and organizations without which this book would not have been possible. Metadata standardization and creation is a community effort and is always better for collaboration.

We would like to thank the Library of Congress, Getty Vocabulary Program, the Society of American Archivists, the Dublin Core Metadata Initiative, and the Visual Resources Association for their permission to use portions of their publications to help make our introduction to metadata languages clearer and hopefully more useful to the reader.

Special thanks to Diane Hillman, Steven Miller, and Jan Eklund for their support, advice, and insight into the realm of metadata. Murtha Baca's contribution to VRA Core and CCO, and to the understanding of these standards, was also illuminating.

We are especially grateful to the New Mexico State University Library Archives & Special Collections Department for providing us with a rich supply of example images to use in our text.

Lastly, we would like to acknowledge the support of our institutions, the University of New Mexico Libraries and New Mexico State University Library, for their support in the completion of this project.

December 2012

Foreword

The Metadata Manual provides readers with an excellent, concise, and practical workbook for understanding and creating metadata for digital cultural heritage collections. It introduces readers to the meaning and history of metadata, different metadata languages or schemas, and metadata quality control and interoperability. It includes in one easy-to-reference volume the names and definitions of metadata elements from the Dublin Core and VRA schemes, allowing users to work directly from this volume.

In contrast to other books on the topic, this manual especially targets support staff, volunteers, and students involved in metadata creation. It focuses on giving quick, non-technical answers to common questions, especially for beginners. Another special strength of the *Manual* is the inclusion of practical exercises and answers for users to work through and thereby gain practical understanding.

The Metadata Manual provides a welcome addition to the small collection of books aimed at providing working professionals, staff, and assistants with a solid foundation in the basics of metadata for digital resources and sound guidance in its application in practice.

Steven J. Miller
Senior Lecturer, School of Information Sciences,
University of Wisconsin–Milwaukee

Preface

It's probably an understatement to note that the recent past has been particularly interesting for metadata librarians.

I started out as a cataloger, and originally learned about the larger world of metadata as a participant in the first Dublin Core workshop in 1995. The 17 years since have been an incredible journey, and I've learned more in that span of time than I ever imagined I would when I started out (I already knew cataloging—what else could I possibly need?). Part of the reason I was able to learn so much was because, in pursuing the brave new idea of metadata, I ended up meeting an incredibly interesting array of people. They were not necessarily librarians, but many took the time to talk to me about things I wasn't taught as a cataloger, and in the process helped shape my thinking about where we're going, and how to get there. Most of the time I was smart enough to listen, and most of the people I cared to listen to weren't shy about challenging me on my assumptions, a gift I don't always acknowledge as much as I should.

But more recently, as the world of metadata in libraries has been turned upside down, I've shifted some of my focus to teaching—occasionally as adjunct faculty in library schools (and iSchools, as they define themselves today), or in workshops for practicing librarians. Somehow, though, despite the amazing amount of resources available about metadata, beating a path through the resources and opinions (and pure dreck, it must be said) remains pretty daunting. About eight years ago, I designed a two-day workshop, "Metadata Standards and Applications," as part of an ALCTS training initiative, and some of those materials are still in use. Though each section had small group activities to improve understanding and promote discussion, there was never enough time (even with two days) to meet the enormous needs of the attendees, many of whom were at the first stages of learning what they needed to know to make the leap from cataloger to metadata librarian.

I have to say that I enjoy teaching more in a workshop setting than in a regular semester-long class, and I particularly like working with practising librarians, most of whom are eager to learn, persistent in their quest to understand, and happy to come away with whatever map for continuing education is available to them and endorsed by someone they trust. I have also spent time discussing some of these instructional issues with regular faculty teaching classes in cataloging, or metadata, or both. The issues that come up time and again are very similar to those heard when cataloging was still the most important skill: what do librarians need to know, and how do you cope with the tension between old and new, the abstract ideas and the concrete skills? The answers vary as much as the personalities represented, but one thing is clear—many of the teachers are having trouble keeping up too, and are increasingly questioning the value of teaching concrete skills in an environment where employment opportunities for librarians continue to expand beyond the old certainties.

A couple of years ago, I designed a "virtual" course for the University of Washington iSchool focusing on the topic of "RDA as data." For me it was a considerable leap: I'd never done an online course, and, though I knew that topic very well, the resources available were all over the map—in blogs, discussion list posts, and the occasional article in web publications. The course was a mixed success: some of the students ran with it and got a lot out of the experience (one even told me it changed her goals about what she wanted to do as a librarian), but others were clearly in over their heads. The surprise for me (and for her, I think) was that among the stars of the class was someone who had no cataloging background at all and was probably the eldest in the class. So much for assumptions.

As a long-time trainer, I see several problems at the top of this heap of issues, particularly for those whose needs are primarily in continuing education. There aren't a lot of continuing education opportunities available for practising librarians, and the current economic situation has drastically reduced their number. There are also the folks working in smaller or geographically isolated settings, often without a cohort available to them to make group training economically possible. For those librarians working in larger institutional settings or in urban areas where consortial arrangements for training often fill the gaps, the needs are not as dire, but are still there.

Many see webinars as the wave of the future—they're normally cheap to present, with few expenses for the presenting agency. Some organizations make them available at low fees, and encourage sites with a number of participants to pay a somewhat larger group fee and stream the webinar to their group in a local conference room or auditorium setting. Even as webinars have become more mainstream (and the relatively small cohort of well-known presenters have gotten more savvy), registration costs have inevitably risen, but the essential experience at both ends of the computer has remained much the same. For the audience and the speaker, the experience is very limited. The audience generally has access to a chat box to ask questions, but very few do (except if they're having technical problems). For the speaker, who is probably used to speaking to people they can see, it's like speaking into the void—there's no way to check the faces of the people in the front row to see if you're getting your point across, and you can't pay attention to the questions because it's so easy to lose the thread of the presentation by doing so. Yes, I can do the webinar in my jammies if I want, but the result is that in almost all cases the lack of interaction and feedback makes the experience less than satisfying for all parties.

Clearly the needs for continuing education, both in group settings and individually, are not being met, particularly in an environment where the pace and extent of change are continual. These enormous needs are unlikely to be met if the only support we can offer our colleagues is lists of readings and the occasional in-person presentation, webinar, or hallway conversation. Some of the needs are certainly still for a better overall understanding of the environment of change in which we live, which can sometimes be met by the increasing availability of screencasts, video recordings, and webinars using well-regarded speakers, plus the usual articles and conference papers. The more pressing of these needs are in the reinforcement of the abstract knowledge with more concrete application of that knowledge. Catalogers, in particular, have expressed a great deal of frustration about the lack of hands-on learning opportunities, which cannot be met even in all-day events at the major library conferences. The "sage on the stage" events are important, surely, but primarily at the early stages of learning, when knowing-what-you-don't-know is the most important goal. After that, there needs to be something else, some additional learning options, that reinforce those new ways of looking at things.

With this background, I was happy to hear about the approach for this book, which seeks to address that need. This is very good news, and I well understand the challenge undertaken by the authors. As catalogers, we have been accustomed to working in an environment where there are approved answers to most questions of application of standards to a variety of situations. This is no longer a feature of the world we're facing. Not only are relevant standards emanating from a variety of organizations—many of them relatively unknown in the library world—but there has been little experience with these standards in LibraryLand. Even when there is some experience to draw on, it tends not to be packaged with guidance or examples that make sense to librarians, who tend to expect a level of congruence between standards that does not yet—and may never—exist.

The case of the eXtensible Markup Language (XML) is a good example. This standard, currently under the purview of the World Wide Web Consortium (W3C), has been around for some time and is ubiquitous as an encoding standard on the web and in any domain where data sharing is necessary. (It's also used widely as a document mark-up language, but that's a topic for another day.) To use and share XML, an XML schema is necessary, because XML is, in reality, simply a packaging format, and the schema makes the contents of that package understandable by others—particularly machines—by referring to external sources of information about how the data is defined and structured. The XML schema makes it possible for data packaged in XML to be validated and to be easily transformed using the eXtensible Stylesheet Language Transformations (XSLT) to move between one XML representation and another as part of a processing routine.

MARC has had an XML version, distributed by the Library of Congress, for over a decade, originally defined with a DTD (Document Type Definition), now replaced by an XML schema. MARCXML is generally used as a first processing step as a way to translate from MARC's native format into something more up-to-date, and the MARC21XML site (*http://www.loc.gov/standards/marcxml*) maintains links to a variety of tools and XSLT scripts developed over time by the Library of Congress and others to provide ways for libraries with available IT resources to work with MARC more easily.

One of the transformations available on that page is between MARCXML and LC's more current recommended set of elements, the Metadata Object Description Schema (MODS) (*http://www.loc.gov/standards/mods*). MODS was originally called "MARC Lite," and was designed by LC as a more modern version of MARC, and, indeed, taking a look at MODS reveals its MARC "bones" as clearly as an X-ray does. One difference is that the labels within the XML < > containers are not expressed as MARC numeric tags, but as English words (which was criticized at the time as a step back from a more international view). Another, more important, difference is that MODS no longer reflects MARC very well, as the MODS developers (working on their own for the first years) built in some additional "features" that are often considered poor practice in metadata circles, and MODS has been evolving separately for most of its existence.

A short history of these descriptions should give some indication of why the metadata world is not an easy one to figure out or follow easily. Keep in mind that, only a few years ago, most metadata-watchers still believed that it was necessary to choose between the available packages of element sets or property sets (sometimes called "metadata schemas"), and come up with one that best met the needs of a project, institution, etc. Now it's not so simple, as the proliferation of choices continues to increase, and the advent of Application Profiles makes it possible to mix-and-match, so long as you expose what you're doing to the people who might want to use your data.

Things are likely to get even more interesting over the next few years, as the big players make adjustments to their business plans and priorities and even more players—big and small—enter the fray. For instance, as libraries continue to hear the siren call of Linked Open Data, the idea that libraries might want to use other people's data and not just expose ours for the use of others has made our world even more complex. Many librarians know that Wikipedia has its own data format (known as dbpedia), which is widely used on the web—and, incidentally, has begun to use Virtual International Authority File (VIAF) links. Last year it was primarily Resource Description and Access (RDA) and its use of the Functional Requirements for Bibliographic Records (FRBR) that held our collective attention, but about a year ago the Library of Congress announced the Bibliographic Framework Transition Initiative (BibFrame, *http://www.loc.gov/marc/transition/*), whose stated goal is to "replace MARC." Outside the library community, the companies in charge of the major search engines (Google, Yahoo, Microsoft, etc.) got together to create their own metadata property set, commonly known as Schema.org (*http://schema.org*). Lest you think that this effort only has relevance for commercial metadata, consider that the first iteration of OCLC's linked data that was exposed and generally available included several Schema.org properties, but none from RDA.

My purpose here was not to frighten you, but to encourage you to take charge of your own learning, either individually or in groups, and ramp up your personal educational plan. Don't wait for all this to "settle down" or be "finished"—neither is likely to happen. There is no promise (or suggestion) by those already up to their eyeballs in this effort (including me) that anything is going to get simpler any time soon. And we're not going back, no matter how attractive that proposition seems sometimes. The good news is that all of you reading this book have made a commitment to learn more, and I salute you!

Diane I. Hillmann
Partner, Metadata Management Associates
Vocabulary Maintenance Officer, Dublin Core Metadata Initiative
October, 2012

About the authors

Amy S. Jackson is the Performing Arts and Digital Arts Librarian at the University of New Mexico (UNM). Prior to this position, she was a Digital Initiatives Librarian at UNM, where she managed the institutional repository and other digital projects. Her previous employers include the University of Illinois at Urbana Champaign, Indiana State University, and Harvard College Libraries. Amy's research interests focus on making electronic resources findable through quality metadata, a topic that has held her interest since her position as Project Coordinator of the IMLS Digital Collections and Content project at the University of Illinois at Urbana Champaign. She received her MLIS from Simmons College in Boston, and also holds a master's degree in music from the Peabody Conservatory of Johns Hopkins University.

Rebecca L. Lubas is Director, Discovery, Acquisitions, and Consortial Services at the University of New Mexico Libraries. Rebecca was previously Head of Cataloging and Metadata Services and Special Formats Cataloger at the Massachusetts Institute of Technology (MIT) Libraries, and a founding member of the Metadata Services Unit at MIT. Rebecca has focused on visual and electronic resources since the beginning of her career. Rebecca holds an MA in English Literature from Ball State, an MLIS from Louisiana State University, and a BA from the University of Notre Dame, USA. She is the editor of *Practical Strategies for Cataloging Departments*.

Ingrid Schneider is the Metadata and Authority Control Librarian at New Mexico State University, where she has been working to lay the foundation for a dedicated digital initiatives unit within the University Library, and to build the Library's inaugural digital collections. Her professional interests include systems librarianship as related to digital collections, and the provision of training in metadata production in all types of institutions. Ingrid received her MLS from Indiana University, and holds Bachelor's Degrees in English and German from Ohio University.

Introduction to metadata

Abstract: This chapter outlines the function, history, and types of metadata used in libraries and other cultural heritage institutions. The history of library metadata, its development in relation to the evolution of information technology, and its importance to later metadata schemas is put in context. The chapter also looks at the importance of metadata to digital resources, as well as how metadata improves the discovery of resources. Types of metadata such as descriptive metadata and rights metadata are distinguished. This chapter also presents an example of Dublin Core metadata expressed in XML. Also included is a discussion of consistency and quality control. Common metadata languages are discussed, and resources for more information are listed for the most commonly used metadata languages in cultural heritage institutions.

Key words: Cataloging, metadata, discovery, descriptive metadata, administrative metadata, rights metadata.

Introduction

Congratulations! If you are reading this book, you have probably decided that metadata is important to you, but you have to go about figuring how to do it. Perhaps you are starting a collection of digital images from scratch. Perhaps you have inherited a collection to curate, but the person who set up the system for metadata creation failed to leave you any documentation. You don't have the time or the funds to go to a workshop lasting a week, let alone to take a semester-long course. You need to create quality metadata NOW. My colleagues and I decided to create this metadata workbook because your plight is very common. Much of the material in this book evolved from our "Metadata Day" workshop, which we presented around New Mexico and West Texas, to cultural heritage professionals just like you. Their participation and feedback helped inform the format of this workbook.

The metadata manual: how to use

Our goal is to give the reader a flexible how-to guide, and to provide enough background and practice to understand the context and utility of several popular metadata languages. You can read the whole book in order, or pick out the chapters on metadata languages that you need to know.

If you choose to focus on specific languages, we suggest reading this chapter, to give you background and history, as well as the XML chapter before going further. Although you may not need to create metadata directly in XML, since it is the foundation of data exchange on the web, having a working knowledge of it may help you better understand and interact with data.

To begin

In this first chapter we will begin with the basics, to give you some grounding in the function of metadata before we look more closely at the specifics of the metadata languages you are most likely to need in a cultural heritage institution.

This chapter should help you:

- gain an understanding of the purpose and utility of metadata;
- learn about the history of metadata development;
- understand why metadata is vital in the digital world;
- learn the vocabulary associated with some of the most common metadata languages and understand when you would want to use them;
- know where to find more information.

What is metadata?

An often-quoted definition of metadata is "data about data." This is a literal definition, but perhaps not the most illuminating. In 2004, the

National Information Standards Organization (NISO) defined metadata as "structured information that describes, explains, locates, or otherwise makes it easier to retrieve, use, or manage an information resource" (NISO, 2004, p. 1).

The Federal Geographic Data Committee (FGDC), in its "Business Case for Metadata," has a helpful description of metadata. Although it focuses on geographic information, the statement applies to all metadata:

> Metadata helps people who use [geospatial] data find the data they need and determine how best to use it. Metadata supports producers in locating and using their own data resources and data consumers in locating and using data resources produced by others. (FGDC, 2012)

Try to think of metadata as a piece of information describing a resource. It's like the nutritional information on a package of food – metadata is the information about what's inside the package. You can also think of the information that you enter into a social networking site such as Facebook or LinkedIn as metadata about yourself. Metadata can describe a wide variety of information, such as:

- the subject matter of the resource;
- the creators of the resource;
- the technical information needed to store and access the resource;
- the legal rights to the resource.

Metadata can be used to find, gather, and maintain resources over long periods of time. Think about all the information that a user will need to know whether the resource meets their needs and whether and how they can use it. Metadata can tell you what the information is about, how to use it, whether you need permission to use it, and where to get that information. Metadata makes web searching more meaningful. It helps you promote your resources, reach the right audience, and make connections between related resources.

Another question about metadata: Why do it? After all, there are powerful search engines readily available and many resources are full-text searchable. However, many resources are not text. Image files would be undiscoverable on the web without textual metadata describing the image. Even in a text resource, some important information may not be easily available. The author may not be clearly stated, or the sponsoring institution, or the copyright owner. All are areas of sufficient concern for libraries and cultural heritage institutions to justify metadata production.

Unfortunately, metadata is often perceived as being a fussy, labor-intensive, unnecessary step in data management. Lynda Wayne of the FGDC identifies the perceived major obstacles to metadata creation (Wayne, 2005, p. 1):

- Metadata standards are too expensive and difficult to implement.
- Metadata production requires time and other resources.
- There are few immediately tangible benefits and incentives to produce metadata.

These perceptions require that we make metadata creation as efficient as possible, promote the benefits of metadata, and publicize results. Time and care at the stage of creating workflows will pay off when you can report how impact on workload is reduced. Promotion of metadata shouldn't end with the creation of metadata, but we need to keep telling our administrations and resource providers how metadata is increasing visibility of collections. Keeping statistics on the usage of the collection, especially if you have pre- and post-metadata enrichment figures, can make a compelling case.

History of metadata

Metadata, by any other name, has been around as long as libraries and archives. Library cataloging is descriptive metadata. The earliest catalogs were "dictionary catalogs"– manuscript or printed volumes with entries describing the material in the collection. Any inventory of books, documents, or objects could be considered descriptive metadata. As collections grew, these inventories needed to become more systematized. Understanding some background and history of library cataloging evolution can be helpful in knowing where some metadata conventions have their roots, and why there are so many metadata "crosswalks" involving library standards.

"Classic" library cataloging, which dates back to antiquity, was primarily focused on description of content. Cataloging described the creator of the resource (usually a book), the title, the physical characteristics of the resource, and the subject matter. The dictionary catalogs of earlier centuries evolved into card catalogs as libraries grew, providing an easy way to file more titles without having to republish the catalog too frequently. Subject analysis also became necessarily more complex. The amount of information in collections was growing, so organizing the material for browsing became a more complicated task.

While there were many predecessor systems for creating library cataloging, the most ubiquitous today is the pairing of MARC 21 and AACR2 – the Anglo-American Cataloging Rules, revision 2, expressed in MAchine-Readable Cataloging tags. This is the cataloging you see in most Integrated Library Systems (ILSs), and up until very recently was the only metadata standard in them. The first edition of AACR was published in 1967, and there were major revisions in 1978, 1988, and 2002, with many updates in between revisions. MARC was developed in the 1960s and became an international standard in 1973. MARC was necessary because, while descriptions, subject analysis, and classification could exist in dictionaries or on cards in "naked" form, albeit in an order, data within a machine needs a container.

A key reason for the universality of MARC/AACR2 is their usage by the Library of Congress (LC). Because so many American libraries (and a significant number of international libraries) use LC data to populate their catalogs, the standards that LC uses are adopted widely. Even before MARC and ILSs, the cards distributed by LC could be considered the first shareable metadata. The development of the database and bibliographic utility services built by the Online Computer Library Center (OCLC) in the early 1970s made sharing MARC records between libraries very efficient, even more so than waiting to receive a shipment of catalog cards, which was how records were shared before the MARC standard and adoption of ILSs. There are now billions of descriptive bibliographic records in this format, contributed by libraries all over the world, not only the English-speaking world.

With the wider availability of the ILS in the 1980s and later, other types of library metadata became more uniform, even though they were not as prescribed as the descriptive metadata. Acquisitions metadata, such as order records and check-in records for serials, laid a foundation for access and rights metadata. Circulation metadata, while it helped libraries as an inventory and management feature, also built up stores of personal metadata in the form of patron records. All of this decades before Facebook!

As new formats for information emerged, especially electronic ones, the rules for description needed to evolve. As AACR was revised, it included more formats. But the standard remained centered on the needs and viewpoint of the library community. The special collections, archives, and image community began developing separate standards, such as Descriptive Cataloging for Rare Materials and the Simons-Tansey classification for images in slide collections.

In the 1990s, things began to change drastically. The growth in size, popularity, and availability of the internet, along with the ongoing improvement of the ILS, the advent of web-based user interfaces, and increased access to databases, meant that metadata could be linked, cross-referenced, and aggregated more easily than before. At the same time, data storage became cheaper and there was an explosion in the amount of information being produced and the speed at which it could be distributed. The next logical step in this evolution was the gathering of born-digital and digitized materials into aggregations of digital library data from collections around the world. But, in order for this to be successful, it is essential that cultural heritage professionals have a firm understanding of the structure and the variety of types of the metadata that evolved in response to the recent, rapid changes in the technological landscape.

The next edition of AACR, Resource: Description and Access (RDA), is considered a new standard, not just a new edition. In 2013, the Library of Congress and libraries participating in the Program for Cooperative Cataloging will migrate from AACR2 to RDA, but for the near future RDA metadata will still be expressed in the MARC standard. Today some ILSs can display the popular Dublin Core metadata standard, but many libraries keep to AACR2/MARC in their main catalogs and use other standards only in digital repositories. In fact, many libraries will still duplicate metadata originating in a non-MARC format in their main library catalog in MARC, because their record of AACR2/MARC metadata is comprehensive and cross-platform searching is not yet completely seamless. Duplicating the metadata in MARC allows users to search one data set expressed in one standard. The MARC standard evolved to answer a specific need in library cataloging, and, despite ongoing efforts to find a replacement, it persists in thousands of library catalogs in literally billions of records. Any successor to MARC will still need to reckon with it.

The types and structure of metadata

Metadata records are composed of three pieces: syntax, structure, and semantics. The syntax is the encoding standard. It functions as both a

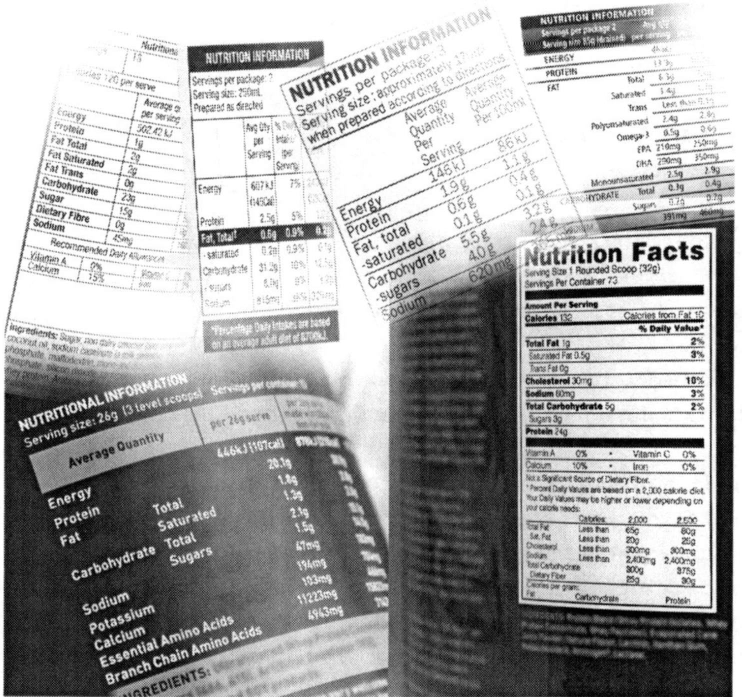

Figure 1.1 **Nutrition information**

Image Copyright 2012, Les Cunliffe

container for the structure and semantics and a set of rules by which the contents should be interpreted. RDF (Resource Description Framework), XML (eXtensible Markup Language), XHTML (eXtensible HyperText Markup Language), and DHTML (Dynamic HyperText Markup Language) are all examples of encoding standards. All can be used to contain the metadata related to cultural heritage objects, although RDF and XML (which will be discussed in the next chapter) are most commonly used in this context. Below, the same record is represented in two different formats (Figure 1.1). The first example is expressed without encoding and the second example includes XML encoding.

Title: Nutrition information
Creator: Cunliffe, Les
Subject: Nutrition; Food--Labeling
Description: Image shows a montage of nutrition labels taken from different food packaging.

Publisher:
Date: 2012-04-03
Type: Still Image
Format: image/jpeg
Identifier: 40433994
Source: Fotolia.com
Relation:
Rights: Copyright 2012, Les Cunliffe

```
<?xml version="1.0" encoding="UTF-8"?>
<oai_dc:dc
  xsi:schemaLocation="http://www.openarchives.org/OAI/2.0/
oai_dc/#x2003;http://www.openarchives.org/OAI/2.0/oai_dc.
xsd">
  <dc:title>Nutrition information</dc:title>
  <dc:creator>Cunliffe, Les</dc:creator>
  <dc:subject>Nutrition; Food--Labeling</dc:subject>
  <dc:description>Image shows a montage of nutrition
labels taken from different food packaging</dc:
description>
  <dc:publisher></dc:publisher>
  <dc:date>2012-04-03</dc:date>
  <dc:type>Still Image</dc:type>
  <dc:format>image/jpeg</dc:format>
  <dc:identifier>40433994</dc:identifier>
  <dc:source>Fotolia.com</dc:source>
  <dc:relation></dc:relation>
  <dc:rights>Copyright 2012, Les Cunliffe</dc:rights>
</oai_dc:dc>
```

The structure fits inside the syntax and is composed of a metadata scheme. Dublin Core, Visual Resources Association (VRA) Core 4.0, Categories for the Description of Works of Art (CDWA) Lite, and Encoded Archival Description (EAD) are all examples of structures. While the encoding standard gives a computer system the instructions on how to interpret the record as a whole, the structure gives humans instructions on how to interpret the information within individual tags (e.g. creator, title, subject, etc.). You can think of structure standards as prescribed tag labels (but not the content of the tags). Below, the structure standard (Dublin Core) is bolded:

```
<?xml version="1.0" encoding="UTF-8"?>
<oai_dc:dc
  xsi:schemaLocation="http://www.openarchives.org/OAI/2.0/
oai_dc/  http://www.openarchives.org/OAI/2.0/oai_dc.xsd">
  <dc:title>Nutrition information</dc:title>
  <dc:creator>Cunliffe, Les</dc:creator>
  <dc:subject>Nutrition; Food--Labeling</dc:subject>
  <dc:description>Image shows a montage of nutrition
labels taken from different food packaging</dc:
description>
  <dc:publisher></dc:publisher>
  <dc:date>2012-04-03</dc:date>
  <dc:type>Still Image</dc:type>
  <dc:format>image/jpeg</dc:format>
  <dc:identifier>40433994</dc:identifier>
  <dc:source>Fotolia.com</dc:source>
  <dc:relation></dc:relation>
  <dc:rights>Copyright 2012, Les Cunliffe</dc:rights>
</oai_dc:dc>
```

The final piece of a metadata record is the semantics, or content standards. Content standards define how the information within the tags should be formatted. Formatting instructions include where periods and commas should be placed, how titles should be formatted (placement of semicolon before subtitle), order of names (last, first), etc. In libraries, AACR2 (Anglo-American Cataloging Rules, Second Edition) is the most commonly used content standard. VRA Core 4.0 uses CCO (Cataloging Cultural Objects) as a content standard. Using content standards ensures the uniformity of the information contained within the tags, which is an essential piece of producing high-quality, interoperable metadata in our text-dominated world.

```
<?xml version="1.0" encoding="UTF-8"?>
<oai_dc:dc
  xsi:schemaLocation="http://www.openarchives.org/OAI/
2.0/oai_dc/ http://www.openarchives.org/OAI/2.0/oai_dc.
xsd">
  <dc:title>Nutrition information</dc:title>
  <dc:creator>Cunliffe, Les</dc:creator>
  <dc:subject>Nutrition; Food--Labeling</dc:subject>
  <dc:description>Image shows a montage of nutrition
```

```
labels taken from different food packaging</
dc:description>
  <dc:publisher></dc:publisher>
  <dc:date>2012-04-03</dc:date>
  <dc:type>Still Image</dc:type>
  <dc:format>image/jpeg</dc:format>
  <dc:identifier>40433994</dc:identifier>
  <dc:source>Fotolia.com</dc:source>
  <dc:relation></dc:relation>
  <dc:rights>Copyright 2012, Les Cunliffe</dc:rights>
</oai_dc:dc>
```

There are different types of metadata that fit within the structure and syntax of a metadata record. Descriptive metadata can be divided into three distinct classes – description, classification, and subject analysis. We've already discussed the history of description above. Classification schemes, such as the widely recognized (and still used) Dewey Decimal System, Library of Congress classification, and Universal Decimal Classification, collate information resources and provide physical addresses for printed and other physical materials on the shelf. In online catalogs, classification is still used in classification browse searches by advanced library users.

Controlled vocabularies developed to aid subject-focused research. In addition to the familiar library controlled vocabularies such as Library of Congress Subject Headings and Sears Subject Headings, specialized vocabularies have been developed to fill the description needs of specialized disciplines. The Getty Thesaurus of Art and Architecture was developed for use in art and museum collections to more deeply describe eras and styles of art. Many museum collections and other cultural heritage institutions use this thesaurus, finding it more definitive for their needs than a general library vocabulary.

In contrast, free-text "tags" are popular on common social media and information sharing sites, such as photo-sharing sites. There are no mandated lists to choose from, unless the user self-imposes one. In this context, tags are keywords that the user applies. Tags can have their place within more structured metadata, especially if the repository owner wishes to promote the content via social media.

While descriptive metadata is very useful, telling us what the subject matter of an object is, describing its form, and telling us who created it, there are other aspects of a resource that need metadata. In the electronic information world, technical metadata is a necessity. Technical metadata tells how the resource was created, how it is stored and preserved, and what system specifications you need to use it. Because technology is evolving so quickly, technical metadata is essential to ensure continuing access to resources as the technology that contains them ages.

Administrative metadata tells who or what owns and/or maintains the item. This type of metadata first appeared in the archives world, where aspects of information such as provenance were important to the history and context of a resource. Because of the ease of reuse of digital information, having administrative metadata to track the lifecycle and usage of the resource is more universally important than before.

The easy transfer and reuse of digital content has increased the importance of rights metadata as well. Rights metadata describes copyright and the terms of use of the resource described. In the print realm, a copyright statement in the verso of the title page usually was sufficient to address this information need. But, in the electronic world, rights are not always as clear, and, since pieces of information are unbound, uncoupled, and mashed up, information about rights needs to be intrinsically bound to the data.

While it can protect intellectual property ownership, rights metadata can also aid in the use of a resource. While you might want to protect your ownership of an item, you may also want people to use and reuse it, and expose your idea or image in other venues. While, of course, there is much careless reuse of material on the internet, legitimate scholars and researchers will only use items that they can properly cite. If you clearly state your rights to the information, and include a Creative Commons-style license granting the right to use your work as long as it is properly cited, you can actually increase the chances that your work will be used – scholars will feel comfortable that they have done due diligence and the work or idea is cleared to be used.

As a cultural heritage institution, you want your information and material to be exposed in this way – you're an information provider, not an information hoarder. Judicious use of rights metadata will help expose your collections to a wider audience.

"Metadata is key to ensuring that resources will survive and continue to be accessible into the future" (NISO, 2012, p. 1). It will also lead researchers to your collections of content.

Metadata languages

In this book, we're going to provide lessons and exercises in the metadata languages you will most commonly encounter in the cultural heritage realm. The most common metadata languages became that way because they were incorporated in popular content management systems, and, as more content management systems adopted them, more systems could "talk" to each other. If you have a working knowledge of these languages, you can converse with much of the digital cultural heritage world.

To give you some idea of the usage of these languages, in her 2009 Association of Research Libraries (ARL) survey, Ma reports that, while the MARC format is the most widely used metadata schema (91 percent), it is followed by EAD (84 percent), Unqualified Dublin Core (DC) (78 percent), and Qualified DC (67 percent) (Ma, 2009, p. 5).

The eXtensible Markup Language (XML) is the all-purpose container language behind much information on the web. You do not need to memorize lines and lines of code to use XML; there are tools out there to help you with that. Being familiar with XML will give you a solid foundation for metadata work. We will discuss this markup language in detail in our next chapter.

Dublin Core is a common descriptive metadata language that was developed in the library community in the mid-1990s and has since seen wide adoption. Its simplicity and flexibility allow quick adoption and easy crosswalking to other metadata languages. Subsequently, Dublin Core has become the base metadata scheme for many platforms. We'll be covering Dublin Core in depth in Chapter 3, since you are very likely to encounter it and use it.

EAD was developed to address the complex relationships in manuscript collections. Since many cultural heritage institutions have manuscript collections, we will explore EAD in Chapter 4.

In many of our institutions, images are our most precious content, and availability opportunities have never been better with web storage and sharing technology. We will cover two standards that are essential to providing useful metadata for images: CDWA and VRA Core 4.0. CDWA provides a means for describing and accessing information about works of art, architecture, other material culture, groups and collections of works, and related images (Getty, 2009). VRA Core provides an element set that can be used by itself to describe visual resources, and in conjunction with other standards. These two languages together describe images in a more powerful and useful way than previously available in print-centered descriptive methods. Chapters 5 and 6 will give you the opportunity to learn more about these schemas and try exercises using them.

Quality control and interoperability

> Describing a resource with metadata allows it to be understood by both humans and machines in ways that promote interoperability. Interoperability is the ability of multiple systems with different hardware and software platforms, data structures, and interfaces to exchange data with minimal loss of content and functionality. (NISO, 2004, p. 4)

Consistency is key to allowing discovery to happen in the digital world. Users don't want to search one system at a time; they want to search across platforms. Metadata can help achieve seamless access to information.

You may find yourself needing to convince administration of the value of metadata creation. Lynda Wayne of the FDGC provides helpful suggestions for convincing administration and staff of the value of metadata which you can use if you need to justify metadata creation to an audience. Metadata aids in the archiving, assessment, discovery, transfer, and distribution of your valuable resources (Wayne, 2005, p. 5).

Make metadata creation part of your processes. Use project "punch lists" that indicate work is not complete until the metadata is complete (Wayne, 2005, p. 7). If you are a solo librarian or curator, making metadata part of the process for yourself will maximize efficiency.

We hope you are already convinced of the tangible benefits to your user community. With this workbook, we hope to break down some key standards so you find them manageable, the implementation is eased, and you can minimize the time and resources spent on this important activity. Because metadata languages will continue to evolve as the way people interact with information continues to evolve, we hope that this workbook will also give you a basic metadata familiarity that will aid you in keeping current with future metadata developments. Keeping current and keeping flexible are vital to continuing to provide quality data that can be discovered, used, and reused.

Where to go for more information

This workbook will focus on Dublin Core, XML, CDWA, VRA, and EAD in more depth since they are the metadata languages you are most likely to need in digital repositories for cultural heritage institutions. Here are some organizations that provide metadata standards if you need more information, or more subject-specific metadata schemas:

- *Creative Commons*

  The Creative Commons' website at *http://creativecommons.org/licenses/by-nc/3.0/us/* contains licenses that you can use in rights metadata to suit your institutions' needs for declaring ownership and granting rights.

- *FDGC*

  The Federal Geographic Data Committee was an early proponent of the implementation of metadata creation. Metadata is especially critical to geospatial data sets, because if you don't have the parameters of the data set recorded you can't create a reliable map. While you are only likely to use FDGC if you have geospatial data in abundance, their materials are worth looking at if you need to write a justification for metadata work. Many of their points can be generalized to other types of data.

  See *http://www.fgdc.gov/library*

- *The Getty Institute*
- In addition to CDWA, the Getty Institute provides many useful tools for metadata creation. The popular Getty Art & Architecture Thesaurus (AAT) is just one of the subject vocabularies they maintain. The Getty also maintains Cultural Objects Name Authority list (CONA), The Getty Thesaurus of Geographic Names (TGN), and the Union List of Artist Names (ULAN). The Getty resources are essential if you are working with an art collection.

  See *http://www.getty.edu/research/tools/vocabularies/*

- *Library of Congress*

  The Library of Congress is still the go-to source for library cataloging, and will be for some time to come despite all the rising competition. The Library of Congress maintains policy statements for interpreting AACR2 and the Library of Congress Classification (LCC) and the Library of Congress Subject Headings (LCSH). You will encounter Library of Congress data if you interact with libraries regularly. LCSH is not only useful because of its popularity; it is also comprehensive. If your collection has a wide focus the LCSH can be a good choice, and users will find the format familiar.

- *MARC (Machine Readable Cataloging) and Crosswalking*

  Even if you are not working in a MARC-based cataloging system, you may encounter MARC if you want to use data from a library, or have your data exported to a library.

  The basics of MARC can be found at *http://www.loc.gov/marc/bibliographic/*

  MARC to Dublin Core Crosswalk *http://www.loc.gov/marc/marc2dc.html*

  Getty Multilanguage Crosswalk *http://www.getty.edu/research/conducting_research/standards/intrometadata/crosswalks.html* (includes CDWA, CCO, VRA, Metadata Object Description Schema (MODS), MARC, Describing Archives: A Content Standard (DACS), and EAD)

- *Resource Description and Access (RDA) (and AACR2)*

  RDA was implemented by the Library of Congress and the Program for Cooperative Cataloging in March 2013.

  RDA website *http://www.rda-jsc.org/rda.html*

  The *RDA Toolkit* is a subscription-based resource. If you are working with library cataloging you will need access to this resource. While there is a print version, the standard was designed to be an online tool and the print version does not work well for referring between sections. See *http://www.rdatoolkit.org/* for more information.

  The *RDA Vocabularies* on the Open Metadata Registry: *http://rdvocab.info*.

2

XML basics

with S.Y. Zoe Chao

Abstract: The goal of this chapter is to give the reader a basic understanding of eXtensible Markup Language, or XML. This will help the reader's ability to learn and use the metadata schemas in the following chapters. XML is a markup language used to store and exchange data behind the scenes, and is known for its simplicity and flexibility. It is an open standard and no special software is required to read or write an XML record. Even though you may never have to create XML records directly, you should be familiar with and able to read an XML record. Example XML records are provided in this chapter.

Key words: XML, eXtensible Markup Language, metadata, encoding, tags.

What is XML?

XML, or eXtensible Markup Language, is the language most metadata is stored in behind the scenes. You might never deal directly with XML while creating metadata because most content management systems provide forms to enter your metadata. They may store the metadata in a database or in XML, and transfer metadata to other systems using XML. Understanding XML will give you a useful foundation for understanding metadata. XML is a universal language and many metadata examples are expressed in XML.

XML was developed from Standard Generalized Markup Language (SGML) as a flexible mark-up language. A mark-up language is a system of annotating a resource that distinguishes the annotations (comments, instructions, etc.) from the content that is intended to be viewed. Historically, publishers marked up texts with printing instructions. This tradition was carried forward into the World Wide Web, and mark-up languages, such as XML and Hyper Text Markup Language (HTML), differentiate instructions for the display of the content from the content itself.

According to the World Wide Web Consortium (W3C),

> Extensible Markup Language (XML) is a simple, very flexible text format derived from SGML (ISO 8879). Originally designed to meet the challenges of large-scale electronic publishing, XML is also playing an increasingly important role in the exchange of a wide variety of data on the Web and elsewhere. (W3C, 2003)

XML is simple and flexible, and an open standard. You can purchase XML editors such as <oXygen/>, or download free software, such as Notepad++, to create XML records. You can even create XML records in simple text editors such as Notepad. However, XML editors give you color-coded syntax and many more features to make debugging XML records much easier than using a simple text editor.

XML is made up of elements and attributes, and uses angle brackets (< >) to separate the elements. An element is also commonly referred to as a field. For example, if you encoded the title of this book in XML, it would look like this:

```
<title>The Metadata Manual</title>
```

As you can see, the element name, "title," is enclosed in the angle brackets to open the element, and follows a / to close the element. You can continue this simple XML record with the authors' names:

```
<author>Rebecca L. Lubas</author>
<author>Amy S. Jackson</author>
<author>Ingrid Schneider</author>
```

XML is so simple and flexible that anything can be an element. As a librarian or cataloger, you can probably see how easy it would be to create a catalog record in XML. We can add the publisher of the book, a date of publication, and a subject to the catalog record, and have a basic XML record for this book:

```
<title>The Metadata Manual: A practical workbook</title>
<author>Rebecca L. Lubas</author>
<author>Amy S. Jackson</author>
<author>Ingrid Schneider</author>
<publisher>Chandos Publishing</publisher>
<date>2013</date>
<subject>Metadata</subject>
```

This is XML at its simplest. This record can be pulled into a database or displayed (using eXtensible Stylesheet Language Transformation, or XSLT) on a web page. For a web display, XSLT tells the browser font size, placement, background color, etc., while XML only carries the text. XML itself does not specify how the elements should be written. For example, XML, or the XML schema you're using, will not tell you if the author's last name should be first or last. It does not tell you how to encode a date, or how much of the title should be in the <title> element. These types of details are specified in content standards such as AACR2, CCO, and DACS (Describing Archives: A Content Standard).

More information about the XML elements can be provided by using attributes. For example, if we want to specify that the subject is from the LCSH, we can use an attribute in the <subject> element.

```
<subject type="LCSH">Metadata</subject>
```

An attribute in the date element could help clarify that the date is a date of publication, and not the date of printing.

```
<date type="publication">2013</date>
```

Attributes always come from a controlled vocabulary defined by the metadata schema that you choose. We'll discuss several metadata schemas later in this book.

As you can see, XML as a container for carrying and transporting metadata is very simple and flexible. However, for XML to be truly powerful, we need to agree on a set of elements, attributes, controlled vocabularies, and encoding standards so that we're all speaking the same language. For example, if I use the element <author>, but someone else uses the element <creator>, the computer will not recognize them as the same concept. Both of us would need to use the same element name. The metadata schema that you choose will define the elements as well as the attributes.

MARCXML, EAD, VRA Core 4.0, and CDWA Lite are metadata schemas created by metadata professionals in the cultural heritage community to define how XML should be used in specific instances. These metadata schemas are represented through machine-readable XML Schema Documents (XSDs) that specify how the schema is to be used. Dublin Core does not include an XSD, but is commonly encoded in XML using the oai_dc XSD for Dublin Core.

How are XML records created?

XML documents are used to transfer data over the internet. XML is text based, so it can be opened with any programs that can read text files. Additionally, an XML file can be created and edited in a simple text editor program, such as Notepad, which is one big advantage of using XML. Here is a simple XML file example:

```
<book>
  Harry Potter
</book>
```

Even though there is only one element here, it is a well-formed XML document. We can name this file "book.xml" or "harrypotter.xml" or others, as long as it's saved as ".xml".

W3C defines an XML element as "everything from (including) the element's start tag to (including) the element's end tag" (W3Schools, 2012). Similarly to HTML, the start tag is presented by two angle brackets: "<" and ">" wrapping around the text: *book*. The end tag of this element will be exactly the same, except adding a slash "/" right after the first angle bracket. And everything between the start and the end tags, including the white space before and between the words, is the content of this element. It can be parsed by the XML parser, which will understand that the text "Harry Potter" is describing a book, not a person. And <book> and </book> are "markup."

In the context of HTML, to markup is to design how the document will display on the browser. The tags in HTML documents are predefined. For example, in HTML, the headings tags <h1>and <h2> designate different font sizes; and content surrounded by paragraph tags, <p>, will have space before and after it. XML tags are not predefined. Not only are you not limited with the aspects of your markup; you can create tags to fit your needs. Therefore, you can mark "Harry Potter" up as:

```
<my_favorite_book>
  Harry Potter
</my_favorite_book>
```

As mentioned above, the white space is part of the element; and it is "character data," just like the string "Harry Potter." Character data, in the context of XML, means the text that is not markup, does not contain any tags. The whitespace before the text is mainly for aesthetics, and mostly ignored by the computer. It is fine if it's written in one line with no space: <my_favorite_book>Harry Potter</my_favorite_book>.

While XML is very flexible and allows you to design your own tags and schema, there are several rules that must be complied with in order to create a well-formed XML document.

Rule 1: Open and Close Tags

In XML, it is essential to have open and close tags balance on either side of the content even if it is an empty element. With empty elements such as </br>, it is acceptable to combine the opening and closing tags into a single element.

Rule 2: Tags are Case Sensitive

It's important to note that, unlike HTML, XML is case sensitive. In HTML, <H1> is the same as <h1>. However, in XML, <book> is not the same as <Book>, and neither is the same as <BOOK>. If the element is started with <book>, you have to close it with </book>; you cannot close it with </Book>.

Rule 3: Tree with One Root

An XML document is structured like a tree. There is a root element at the beginning of every document. As the description of the object goes into more details, it is quite possible the XML will have "branches" formed and "leaves" shaped. Let's use the same example, "Harry Potter." Suppose you would like to add the book's author to your description. You will need to use a more granular markup to differentiate "Harry Potter" and "J K. Rowling." It could look like this:

```
<book>
  <title> Harry Potter</title>
  <author> J K. Rowling</author>
<book>
```

The root element here is <book>, which is the first element in this document that contains all other elements. We can say that <book> is the parent element to both <title> and <author>; and that <title> and <author> are siblings. There will be only one root in every XML document.

In addition to having more tags, another difference you may notice between the first and the second example is that the element <book> has different types of content. In our first example, the content is just text (or character data), "Harry Potter". However, in the second example, the <book> has element contents because it has two child elements. It is common for an XML file to be composed of some elements that have only child elements and some that have only text in the content. It is not against the rules to mix up markups and text within a tag like this:

```
<book>
  <title>Harry Potter</title> is my favorite book written
by <author>J K. Rowling</author>.
</book>
```

In a case like this, we can say that the <book> element contains text and child elements, or "mixed content." Mixed content is common in online articles, reports, and web pages. Because it is harder to parse mixed content in order to extract information, mixed content is much less common in the XML documents that are used for data exchange processes, like the metadata schemas we'll talk about later.

Since only one root element is the parent of all other elements, the structure of the XML document relies on the scope of the subject you want to describe. The root element <book> is suitable if the scope is only one book (Figure 2.1).

However, if the scope is all the books in your collection, you will need to change the root element, for example, <my_library>, in order to encompass all other elements (Figure 2.2).

Certainly, you can start with the smaller content blocks and build up to a bigger structure as you go. However, it is critical to neatly assemble the blocks in a XML document, meaning that the child element needs to be completely enclosed by its parent element.

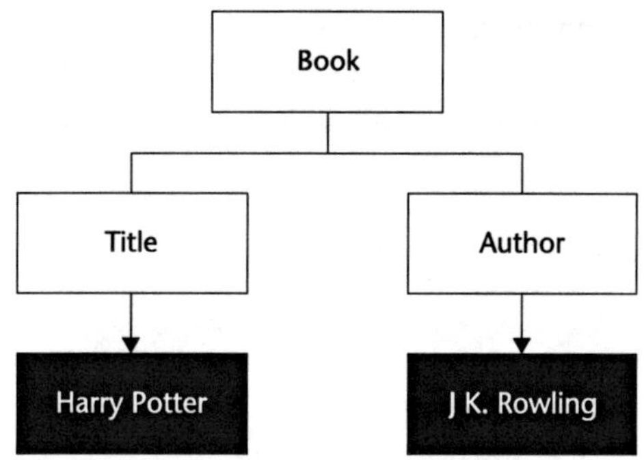

Figure 2.1 <Book> as XML root element

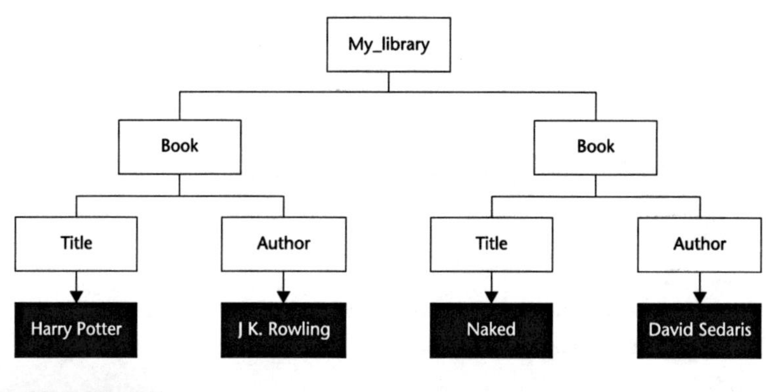

Figure 2.2 <My_library> as XML root element

Rule 4: Elements must be correctly nested

It is not uncommon to see tags overlapping like this in a HTML file:

```
<b><i>The text is bold and italic.</b></i>
```

Often this type of ill-formed HTML document will display in the browser just fine. However, in XML, the open and close tags must nest properly like a Russian doll, or the document will not parse properly. In an XML document, every child can only have one parent. If the start tag of element B is inside the element A, the end tag of element B must also be inside element A. The element A is the only parent of the element B.

```
<A><B>value</B></A>
```

In our example, you must finish describing one aspect of your subject, such as the books you have in your collection, before you can go on to talk about the CDs you have. The trunks and the branches need to have a defined, not a messy, structure.

```
<my_library>
  <books>
    <book>
      <title>Harry Potter</title>
      <author>J K. Rowling</author>
    </book>
    <book>
      <title>Naked</title>
      <author>David Sedaris</author>
    </book>
  </books>
  <CDs>
    <CD>
      <title>Yellow Submarine</title>
      <performer>The Beatles</performer>
    </CD>
    <CD>
      <title>The Essential Duke Ellington</title>
      <performer>Duke Ellington</performer>
    </CD>
  </CDs>
</my_library>
```

Rule 5: Attribute values must be quoted

An attribute is a name-value pair attached to the element's start tag. It can be used to describe the element. Following the previous example, if you would like to differentiate the novels and essays in your book collection, we can add an attribute to the book element:

```
<my_library>
  <books>
    <book category="novel">
      <title>Harry Potter</title>
```

```
    <author>J K. Rowling</author>
  </book>
  <book category="essays">
    <title>Naked</title>
    <author>David Sedaris</author>
  </book>
 </books>
</my_library>
```

You can see that the name of the attribute is separated from the value by an equals sign. The attribute values are enclosed in the quotation marks. For an XML parser, as long as the attribute value is quoted, it does not matter whether a single or a double quotation mark is used. <book category="novel"> means the same as <book category='novel'>. The other rule for the attribute is that no element can have more than one attribute with a given name. For example, it is wrong to have attribute "category" show up twice in the book element, like this:

```
<book category="novel" category="fantasy"> ← wrong
```

You may feel uncertain about when to use an attribute. According to the book "XML in a Nutshell" by Harold and Means, "when and whether one should use child elements or attributes to hold information [is] a subject of heated debate" (2001, p. 16). The rule of thumb is to use attributes only for the information that is not relevant to the data you are describing, because attributes have the following limitations:

- Attributes cannot contain multiple values.
- Attributes cannot contain tree structures.
- Attributes are difficult to read and maintain.
- Attributes are not easily expandable for future changes.

In the previous example, we can pull out the attribute "category" and use it as a child element and solve the problem:

```
<book>
 <category>novel</category>
 <category>fantasy</category>
 <title>Harry Potter</title>
 <author>J K. Rowling</author>
</book>
```

There are situations in which you need to be more specific with the element itself, such as when adding an ID number. In that case, adding attributes is the way to go. In the following example, the id attributes are to differentiate the two book elements; they're not a part of the information of the books themselves.

```
<my_library>
  <books>
    <book id="1">
      <title>Harry Potter</title>
      <author>J K. Rowling</author>
    </book>
    <book id="2">
      <title>Naked</title>
      <author>David Sedaris</author>
    </book>
  </books>
</my_library>
```

You may have noticed that we're using an underscore (_) to bridge multiple words in the element in our examples. That's because element names must not contain a space. However, not all characters are allowed in the element names. We'll talk about that soon, but first we need to talk about some specific characters in the XML document.

Rule 6: Certain characters have a special meaning in XML

Suppose we want to put "< 500 pages" (fewer than 500 pages) in a <page_count> element for the Harry Potter book.

```
<book>
  <title>Harry Potter</title>
  <author>J K. Rowling</author>
  <page_count> < 500 pages</page_count>
</book>
```

A record like this example will generate an error because the "less than" character (<) has a special meaning in XML and will be interpreted as the start of a new tag. So will the characters for "greater than" (>), “ampersand” (&), “apostrophe” (‘), and “quotation mark” (“). Each of these characters means something in the XML syntax. So, instead of using these five characters in our XML document, we will need to replace them with the predefined entity references:

Character	Entity reference	Meaning
<	<	less than
>	>	greater than
&	&	ampersand
‘	'	apostrophe
“	"	quotation

The XML should look like this:

```
<book>
  <title>Harry Potter</title>
  <author>J K. Rowling</author>
  <page_count> &lt; 500 pages</page_count>
</book>
```

Strictly speaking, only the characters “<” and “&” are illegal in XML. The other three will not cause errors, but it is a good practice to replace them with the entity reference.

Rule 7: Proper Element Names

From our examples, we know that English letters, both A to Z and a to z, and “_” (underscore) are allowed. We can use digits 0 through 9, and certainly, in other countries, people can use the characters in their language. However, besides characters “-“ (hyphen) and “.” (period), XML names cannot have other punctuation characters, such as percent symbols, dollar signs, slashes, semicolons, or, of course, quotation marks and apostrophes. Element names must start only with letters or the underscore characters. (Be sure you don’t leave a space between “<” and the element name.) You cannot start an element name with a number, a hyphen, or a period. Also, “xml” (or “XML”, or any case combination) cannot be used as an element name or as the start of an element name.

The following examples are valid element names:

```
<My.Element.Name>
<_element10>
<my-Element>
```

Though you can be creative with the combination of all the legitimate characters within rules, W3C recommends that we follow these best practices for element names:

- Make names descriptive. It's best to use an underscore for two or more words: <first_name>.
- Make names short and simple.
- Avoid "-" and "." Some software may have different interpretations for these two characters.
- Avoid ":" Colons are reserved to be used in namespaces.

Other content in XML

The XML declaration

You may notice that, in metadata examples in this book, the first line of the XML record looks like this:

```
<? xml version="1.0" encoding="UTF-8" standalone="no"?>
```

This is the XML declaration, not an element. It specifies what types of characters are being used for this document and whether this file needs to refer to an external document. The XML declaration is optional; it is recommended by W3C to include it in the beginning of an XML document. When including an XML declaration, you need to make sure that it is at the very beginning of the document; even a single white space before the declaration will cause XML parsing error.

There are three attributes that can be in the XML declaration: version, encoding, and standalone. The version attribute must be included in the declaration. Though there is an XML version 1.1,"1.0" is the only value that you can assign to the version attribute; it will cause parser error otherwise.

By default, the XML document is assumed to be encoded in UTF-8 (Unicode) when the encoding attribute is not specified. We recommend not including an encoding attribute if you are unsure. It causes an error when the attribute specification does not agree with the characters the document uses.

The standalone attribute indicates whether the XML document needs to refer to an external document, such as a DTD (Document Type Definition) or an XSD (XML Schema Document). For the book collection examples we have in this chapter, there are no external files to be referred to, and the standalone will have the value "yes."

```
<?xml version="1.0" encoding="utf-8" standalone="yes"?>
<my_library>
  <books>
    <book>
      <title>Harry Potter</title>
      <author>J K. Rowling</author>
    </book>
    <book>
      <title>Naked</title>
      <author>David Sedaris</author>
    </book>
  </books>
</my_library>
```

The standalone attribute is optional. If it is omitted, the value "no" is assumed.

Comments

Often we need to leave comments in an XML document, either to serve as notes for ourselves or to communicate with co-workers who work on the same file. Similarly to HTML, the comment syntax starts with <!-- and ends with -->. For example:

```
<!-- This is my comment. -->
```

Any characters are allowed in the comments except the double hyphen (--), because it's already used to set aside the comment. Comments can be anywhere in the document except inside a tag, like this:

```
<book <!-- my comment -->>    ← wrong
```

It should be:

```
<book> <!-- my comment -->
   <title>Harry Potter</title>
   <author>J K. Rowling</author>
 </book>
```

CDATA Sections

A CDATA section is the place that allows you to have the character data you don't want to be parsed by the parser in a XML document. Unlike the comments, in which the character data will be completely ignored, the content of CDATA section is still part of the data, but will not be treated as regular XML data. For example, you might want to include a link from Amazon for the book "Harry Potter."

```
<book>
  <title>Harry Potter</title>
  <author>J K. Rowling</author>
  <related_link> http://www.amazon.com/s/&field-
keywords=harry+potter </related_link>
</book>
```

From the XML rules, we learned that "&" needs to be replaced by "&," or there will be a parsing error. However, there is another way to do it: tell the parser not to parse this part of the text.

```
<book>
  <title>Harry Potter</title>
  <author>J K. Rowling</author>
  <related_link>
    <![CDATA[http://www.amazon.
com/s/&field-keywords=harry+potter]]>
  </related_link>
</book>
```

A CDATA section comes in handy when you want to include scripting codes in your XML file, such as this example from W3C:

```
  <script>
 <![CDATA[
     function matchwo(a,b)
     {
     if (a < b && a < 0) then
         {
        return 1;
         }
     else
         {
        return 0;
        }
     }
  ]]>
</script>
```

We don't need to worry about replacing "&" and "<" once we put them inside the CDATA section.

There are two restrictions on CDATA sections. First, "]]>" is not allowed in the CDATA section because it marks the end of the section. Second, you cannot nest a CDATA section inside another CDATA section.

Well-formed vs. valid XML

What we have learned in this chapter will help us to create a well-formed XML document. However, to create a valid XML file, depending on the type of metadata, you will need to follow a specific set of rules, such as a DTD or one of the schemas covered in later chapters. For now, remember to adhere to these rules for well-formed XML documents:

- Open and close elements with angle brackets: <element>text</element>.
- Element names are case-sensitive – these are different: name, Name, NAME, nAmE.
- Structure the document like a tree with one root.
- Elements must be correctly nested.
- Attributes' values must always be quoted.
- Use entity references (<, >, &, ", and ') for these characters: <, >, &, ", '
- Element names must follow the naming guideline.

Why do we use XML?

As you can see, XML is a very simple, flexible, and open format. When used correctly, it's also very powerful.

Open standards are significant in a data-driven environment because this means that your data will not be locked in any proprietary format. A proprietary format relies on specific software to read the data, and could not be read without that software. If, for some reason, the company that created the software disappeared in a few years, and you no longer had access to the software, your data would be locked in that format and lost forever. For example, if you use Microsoft Excel to create and store data, and keep the data in the .xls (or .xlsx) format, only Microsoft Excel will be able to read the data in the future. Other programs (such as Open Office) can often make a guess at what the files say, but, ultimately, only Excel will be able to read all of the data. However, if you save the data as an XML file, almost any program will be able to read it, because XML is an open standard that can be read on multiple platforms. Eric Lease Morgan describes XML as "an open standard providing the means to share data and information between computers and computer programs as unambiguously as possible" (Morgan, 2008).

In the cultural heritage community, standards are important to maintain and follow so that data can be exchanged, shared, and reused. The XML specification is a W3C standard, and, as such, has the support of a significant organization for maintenance and development. By following these standards, the cultural heritage community demonstrates willingness to participate in international standards to share data across domains.

XML also makes it easy to exchange information (records) across platforms and systems. In the libraries, archives, and museums community, a protocol called the Open Archives Initiatives Protocol for Metadata Harvesting (OAI-PMH) is used to pass XML metadata records about items in our collections to other platforms for harvesting and sharing. More information about OAI-PMH is in the last chapter in this book. As soon as XML records are created or harvested, they can be searched across in an XML format using XPath (a language designed for navigating through parts of an XML document), or imported into a database and searched as database records.

Another advantage of XML is its simplicity. Individual communities with special needs can easily create schemas to fit their data, and new standards are easy to share within a community. XML is easy to access and update in bulk; and individual files, especially for descriptive metadata, are small and easy to store.

XML also offers a way to separate data and design. In the libraries, archives, and museum community, we may need access to data, but the way it's displayed is not important. Or, we may want to change the way our data is displayed without having to re-enter all of our data. XML makes this possible.

A final advantage of XML is that multiple applications can use (and reuse) the same data. The data only has to be entered once, and, through the use of XSLT, it can be transformed to fit different environments and needs.

XML example records

Below are examples of the same image cataloged using each of the standards discussed later in this book:

Center for Southwest Research, University Libraries, University of New Mexico

Figure 2.3 **"Bennie"**

Photograph: Lee Marmon Pictorial Collection (PICT 2000-017), Center for Southwest Research, University Libraries, University of New Mexico. 2000-017-0012. Available at: *http://econtent.unm.edu/u?/Marmon,9*

Dublin Core

Dublin Core uses 15 core elements to describe resources.


```
<?xml version="1.0" encoding="UTF-8"?>
<oai_dc:dc xmlns:oai_dc="http://www.openarchives.org/
OAI/2.0/oai_dc/" xmlns:dc="http://purl.org/dc/
elements/1.1/" xmlns:xsi="http://www.w3.org/2001/
XMLSchema-instance" xsi:schemaLocation="http://www.
openarchives.org/OAI/2.0/oai_dc/ http://www.openarchives.
org/OAI/2.0/oai_dc.xsd" >
  <dc:title>Bennie</dc:title>
  <dc:creator>Marmon, Lee</dc:creator>
  <dc:subject>Indians of North America – New Mexico</
dc:subject>
  <dc:description>Portrait of Bennie, with sheep in
background</dc:description>
  <dc:publisher>Center for Southwest Research, University
Libraries, University of New Mexico</dc:publisher>
  <dc:date>1984</dc:date>
  <dc:type>Still image; photograph</dc:type>
  <dc:format>Image/jpeg</dc:format>
  <dc:identifier>2000-017-0012.tif</dc:identifier>
  <dc:source>ZIM CSWR Pict Colls PICT 2000-017
</dc:source>
  <dc:relation>Lee Marmon Pictorial Collection http://
rmoa.unm.edu/docviewer.php?docId=nmupict
2000-017.xml</dc:relation>
  <dc:rights>Copyright of the Lee Marmon Pictorial
Collection has been transferred to the CSWR. No
institutional restrictions placed on use of this
collection. Rights to the digital resource are held by
the University of New Mexico http://www.unm.edu/
disclaimer.html</dc:rights>
  <dc:identifier>http://econtent.unm.edu/u?/Marmon,9</
dc:identifier>
</oai_dc:dc>
```

MARCXML record

Although MARCXML is not discussed in the book, an example record is shown below for those familiar with the MARC standard.

```
<?xml version="1.0" encoding="utf-8"?>
<record xmlns="http://www.loc.gov/MARC21/slim"
xmlns:xsi="http://www.w3.org/2001/XMLSchema-instance"
xsi:schemaLocation="http://www.loc.gov/MARC21/slim
http://www.loc.gov/standards/marcxml/schema/MARC21slim.
xsd">
  <leader> am 3u </leader>
  <datafield tag="042" ind1=" " ind2=" ">
    <subfield code="a">dc</subfield>
  </datafield>
  <datafield tag="720" ind1=" " ind2=" ">
    <subfield code="a">Marmon, Lee</subfield>
    <subfield code="e">author</subfield>
  </datafield>
  <datafield tag="260" ind1=" " ind2=" ">
    <subfield code="c">1984</subfield>
  </datafield>
  <datafield tag="520" ind1=" " ind2=" ">
    <subfield code="a">Portrait of Bennie, with sheep in
background</subfield>
  </datafield>
  <datafield tag="856" ind1=" " ind2=" ">
    <subfield code="q">Image/jpeg</subfield>
  </datafield>
  <datafield tag="024" ind1="8" ind2=" ">
    <subfield code="a">2000-017-0012.tif</subfield>
  </datafield>
  <datafield tag="024" ind1="8" ind2=" ">
    <subfield code="a">http://econtent.unm.edu/u?/
Marmon,9</subfield>
  </datafield>
  <datafield tag="260" ind1=" " ind2=" ">
```

```
    <subfield code="b">Center for Southwest Research,
University Libraries, University of New Mexico</subfield>
  </datafield>
  <datafield tag="787" ind1="0" ind2=" ">
    <subfield code="n">Lee Marmon Pictorial Collection
http://rmoa.unm.edu/docviewer.php?docId=nmupict2000-017.
xml</subfield>
  </datafield>
  <datafield tag="540" ind1=" " ind2=" ">
    <subfield code="a">Copyright of the Lee Marmon
Pictorial Collection has been transferred to the CSWR. No
institutional restrictions placed on use of this
collection. Rights to the digital resource are held by
the University of New Mexico http://www.unm.edu/
disclaimer.html</subfield>
  </datafield>
  <datafield tag="786" ind1="0" ind2=" ">
    <subfield code="n">ZIM CSWR Pict Colls PICT 2000-017</
subfield>
  </datafield>
  <datafield tag="653" ind1=" " ind2=" ">
    <subfield code="a">Indians of North America -- New
Mexico</subfield>
  </datafield>
  <datafield tag="245" ind1="0" ind2="0">
    <subfield code="a">Bennie</subfield>
  </datafield>
  <datafield tag="655" ind1="7" ind2=" ">
    <subfield code="a">Still image; photograph</subfield>
    <subfield code="2">local</subfield>
  </datafield>
</record>
```

Abbreviated EAD record for the Lee Marmon Collection

Note that the EAD record describes the entire collection, not just the single image. Also, this is an abbreviated record. The full record is over 7700 lines. Remember that your software will supply forms for you to enter this information, and very rarely, if ever, will you have to key an entire XML record from scratch.

```
<ead>
  <eadheader findaidstatus="edited-full-draft"
langencoding="iso639-2b" audience="internal"
repositoryencoding="iso15511" countryencoding="iso3166-1"
scriptencoding="iso15924" dateencoding="iso8601"
relatedencoding="Dublin Core">
    <eadid publicid="-//University of New Mexico Center
for Southwest Research//TEXT(US::NmU::PICT 2000-017)//EN"
countrycode="us" mainagencycode="NmU"
encodinganalog="Identifier"/>
    <filedesc>
      <titlestmt>
        <titleproper encodinganalog="Title">Inventory of
the Lee Marmon Pictorial Collection, <date>1936–2010</
date></titleproper>
      </titlestmt>
      <publicationstmt>
        <publisher>University of New Mexico, University
Libraries, Center for Southwest Research</publisher>
        <date era="ce" calendar="gregorian"
encodinganalog="Date">© 2007</date>
          <p>The University of New Mexico</p>
      </publicationstmt>
    </filedesc>
    <profiledesc>
      <langusage>Finding aid is in <language
encodinganalog="Language" langcode="eng">English</
language></langusage>
    </profiledesc>
  </eadheader>
  <archdesc level="collection" relatedencoding="MARC 21">
    <did>
      <head>Collection Summary</head>
      <unittitle encodinganalog="245" label="Title">Lee
Marmon Pictorial Collection</unittitle>
      <unitdate type="inclusive" era="ce" calendar
="gregorian" normal="1936/2008">1936–2010</unitdate>
```

```
     <unitid countrycode="us" label="Collection
Number">PICT 2000-017</unitid>
     <origination label="Creator">
       <persname>Marmon, Lee</persname>
     </origination>
     <physdesc encodinganalog="300" label="Size">
       <extent>36 boxes</extent>
     </physdesc>
     <physloc>B2. Filed by Accession Number.</physloc>
     <repository encodinganalog="852" label=" Repository">
       <corpname>University of New Mexico Center for
Southwest Research</corpname>
     </repository>
     <abstract>This collection contains photographs taken
by Lee Marmon throughout his life. These include images of
elders and community members from Laguna and Acoma Pueblos,
visual documentation of uranium mines and mills throughout
New Mexico, photos of fashion and social life in 1960s and
1970s Palm Springs, CA, among other things.</abstract>
    </did>
    <arrangement>
     <head>Arrangement of the Collection:</head>
     <p>The Lee Marmon Pictorial Collection is arranged
into series: </p>
     <list type="marked">
       <item>Original Lee Marmon Collection (2000)</item>
       <item> American Indian Colleges </item>
       <item>General Photographs</item>
       <item>Moving Images</item>
     </list>
    </arrangement>
    <dsc type="in-depth">
     <head>Contents List</head>
     <c01 level="series">
       <did>
         <unittitle id="orig">ORIGINAL MARMON COLLECTION
(2000)</unittitle>
         <unitdate>1949–1999</unitdate>
       </did>
       <c02 level="file">
         <did>
```

```
          <container type="box">1</container>
          <container type="folder">1</container>
          <unittitle>Portraits – Men </unittitle>
          <unitdate>1949–1963</unitdate>
        </did>
        <scopecontent><p>0001:Lee Marmon with Station
Wagon,1949. 0002: Jeff Sousea "White Man's
Moccasins,"1954. 0003: Gov. James Solomon w/ Lincoln
cane, 1958. 0004: Mateos Mexicano, 1962; 0005: Jose
Sanshu, 1963; 0006: Jose Teofilo, 1961; 0007: Fernando,
1950; 0008: John Riley, 1949</p></scopecontent>
      </c02>
      <c02 level="file">
        <did>
          <container type="box">2</container>
          <container type="folder">1</container>
          <unittitle>Portraits – Men and Women</
unittitle>
          <unitdate>1952–1987</unitdate>
        </did>
        <scopecontent><p>0009: Benson, Navajo
Sheepherder, 1985; 0010: Bronco Martinez,1984; 0011:
Platero, Navajo, 1962; 0012: Bennie, 1984; 0013: Fr.
Kenneth, Acoma, 1952; 0014: Esther – Zuni Pueblo, 1975;
0015: Susie Rayos Marmon, 110th birthday, 1987; 0016:
Lucy Louis – Acoma, 1960</p></scopecontent>
      </c02>
    </c01>
  </dsc>
</ead>
```

VRA Core 4.0 Record

A key feature of VRA Core 4.0 is the ability to distinguish from the original photograph (all elements inside the <work> wrapper) and the digitized image (all elements inside the <image> wrapper).

```
<?xml version="1.0" encoding="UTF-8"?>
<vra xmlns="http://www.vraweb.org/vracore4.htm"
  xmlns:xsi="http://www.w3.org/2001/XMLSchema-instance"
```

```
  xsi:schemaLocation="http://www.vraweb.org/vracore4.htm
http://www.loc.gov/standards/vracore/vra-strict.xsd">
  <work>
    <agentSet>
      <agent>
        <name vocab="NAF" refid="nr 97009000">Marmon, Lee
</name>
        <culture>American</culture>
        <role>photographer</role>
      </agent>
    </agentSet>
    <culturalContextSet>
      <culturalContext>American</culturalContext>
    </culturalContextSet>
    <dateSet>
      <display>1984</display>
      <date type="creation">
        <earliestDate>1984</earliestDate>
        <latestDate>1984</latestDate>
      </date>
    </dateSet>
    <descriptionSet>
      <description>Portrait of Bennie, with sheep in
background</description>
    </descriptionSet>
    <locationSet>
      <location type="creation">
        <name type="geographic" vocab="TGN" refid="7007566"
extent="state">New Mexico</name>
        <name type="geographic" vocab="TGN" refid="7012149"
extent="nation">United States</name>
      </location>
    </locationSet>
    <materialSet>
      <display>black and white film</display>
      <material/>
    </materialSet>
    <measurementsSet>
      <display>4 in (height) × 3.25 in (width)</display>
      <measurements type="height" unit="in">4</measurements>
```

```
      <measurements type="width" unit="in">3.25</
measurements>
    </measurementsSet>
    <relationSet>
      <relation type="partOf">Lee Marmon Pictorial
Collection</relation>
    </relationSet>
    <rightsSet>
      <display>Copyright of the Lee Marmon Pictorial
Collection has been transferred to the CSWR. No
institutional restrictions placed on use of this
collection. Rights to the digital resource are held by
the University of New Mexico http://www.unm.edu/
disclaimer.html</display>
      <rights/>
    </rightsSet>
    <subjectSet>
      <display>Indians of North America -- New Mexico</
display>
      <subject>
        <term type="descriptiveTopic" vocab="LCSH" refid="sh
85065489">Indians of North America -- New Mexico</term>
      </subject>
    </subjectSet>
    <techniqueSet>
      <display>photography</display>
      <technique vocab="AAT" refid="300054225">
photography</technique>
    </techniqueSet>
    <titleSet>
      <display>Bennie</display>
      <title type="descriptive" pref="true" xml:lang=
"en">Bennie</title>
    </titleSet>
    <worktypeSet>
      <display>black-and-white photographs</display>
      <worktype vocab="AAT" refid="300128347">black-and-
white photographs</worktype>
    </worktypeSet>
  </work>
  <image>
```

```
<dateSet>
  <display>2008-11-21</display>
  <date type="creation">
    <earliestDate>2008-11-21</earliestDate>
    <latestDate>2008-11-21</latestDate>
  </date>
</dateSet>
<descriptionSet>
  <description>Created on an Epson Expression 1640XL,
500 ppi, 24 bit</description>
</descriptionSet>
<measurementsSet>
  <display>56.28 KB</display>
  <measurements/>
</measurementsSet>
<relationSet>
  <relation type="imageOf" refid="2000-017-0012"/>
</relationSet>
<rightsSet>
  <display>Copyright of the Lee Marmon Pictorial
Collection has been transferred to the CSWR. No
institutional restrictions placed on use of this
collection. Rights to the digital resource are held by
the University of New Mexico http://www.unm.edu/
disclaimer.html</display>
  <rights/>
</rightsSet>
<techniqueSet>
  <display>digital imaging</display>
  <technique/>
</techniqueSet>
<titleSet>
  <title>Digitized image from photograph</title>
</titleSet>
<worktypeSet>
  <display>digital image</display>
  <worktype/>
</worktypeSet>
</image>
</vra>
```

CDWALite record

CDWALite is primarily used to describe museum resources. This record describes the original photograph.

```
<?xml version="1.0" encoding="UTF-8" standalone="no" ?>
<cdwa:cdwalite xmlns:cdwa="http://www.getty.edu/CDWA/
CDWALite"
  xmlns:xsi="http://www.w3.org/2001/XMLSchema-instance"
  xsi:schemaLocation="http://www.getty.edu/CDWA/CDWALite
http://www.getty.edu/CDWA/CDWALite/CDWALite-xsd-
public-v1-1.xsd">
  <cdwa:descriptiveMetadata>
    <cdwa:objectWorkTypeWrap>
      <cdwa:objectWorkType>photograph
</cdwa:objectWorkType>
    </cdwa:objectWorkTypeWrap>
    <cdwa:titleWrap>
      <cdwa:titleSet>
        <cdwa:title>Bennie</cdwa:title>
      </cdwa:titleSet>
    </cdwa:titleWrap>
    <cdwa:displayCreator>Lee Marmon
</cdwa:displayCreator>
    <cdwa:indexingCreatorWrap>
      <cdwa:indexingCreatorSet>
        <cdwa:nameCreatorSet>
          <cdwa:nameCreator>Marmon, Lee</cdwa:nameCreator>
        </cdwa:nameCreatorSet>
        <cdwa:roleCreator>Photographer</cdwa:roleCreator>
      </cdwa:indexingCreatorSet>
    </cdwa:indexingCreatorWrap>
    <cdwa:displayMaterialsTech>black-and-white
photograph</cdwa:displayMaterialsTech>
    <cdwa:displayCreationDate>1984
</cdwa:displayCreationDate>
    <cdwa:indexingDatesWrap>
      <cdwa:indexingDatesSet>
        <cdwa:earliestDate>1984</cdwa:earliestDate>
        <cdwa:latestDate>1984</cdwa:latestDate>
```

```
      </cdwa:indexingDatesSet>
    </cdwa:indexingDatesWrap>
    <cdwa:locationWrap>
      <cdwa:locationSet>
        <cdwa:locationName>Center for Southwest Research,
University Libraries, University of New Mexico,
Albuquerque, New Mexico</cdwa:locationName>
      </cdwa:locationSet>
    </cdwa:locationWrap>
  </cdwa:descriptiveMetadata>
  <cdwa:administrativeMetadata>
</cdwa:administrativeMetadata>
</cdwa:cdwalite>
```

Example exercise

Create your own XML documents, using a free XML editor (if you don't have one, you can still create an XML document in any text editor). Get comfortable with the coding. Don't worry about following any schemas yet. Schemas will be discussed thoroughly in the following chapters.

3

Using Dublin Core

With information from the Dublin Core Metadata Initiative

Abstract: This chapter describes the history of the Dublin Core Metadata Initiative and the development of the Dublin Core metadata scheme, and provides brief information on changes made to the metadata scheme over time. It includes a discussion of the main principles underlying the standard, definitions of individual properties within the metadata scheme, and guidance in use of the properties for metadata creation. The chapter includes an example of a Dublin Core metadata record, exercises allowing the reader to create Dublin Core metadata, and examples of metadata that could be produced for the exercises.

Key words: Metadata, Dublin Core Metadata Initiative (DCMI), DCMI Metadata Terms, digital images, Online Computer Library Center (OCLC), Simple Dublin Core.

Background/History

Dublin Core is one of the best known and most widespread metadata initiatives. The initial element set, which consisted of 15 core elements, was developed at a joint conference between OCLC (Online Computer Library Center) and NCSA (National Center for Supercomputing Applications) in 1995 in Dublin, Ohio. The impetus for the creation of the element set was the rapid expansion of the internet, the plethora of information that was subsequently becoming available, and recognition that "the Internet ... [would] contain more information than professional abstractors, indexers, and catalogers can manage using existing methods and systems" (Weibel et al., 1995).

The aim and result of the conference was the development of a set of metadata elements that were simple enough for web authors to incorporate into their HTML without needing extensive training in cataloging or indexing (Lagoze, 2001; National Information Standards Organization, 2004, p. 3). The conference also laid the groundwork for the development of the Dublin Core Metadata Initiative: an open, non-profit organization that has maintained and further developed the initial set of metadata elements.

The initial set of metadata elements (there were 15) functioned in the context of three principles: the One-to-One (1:1) principle, the Dumb-Down principle, and the Appropriate Values principle. The One-to-One principle stated that a Dublin Core metadata record should only describe one manifestation or version of a resource. Therefore, in the case of a photo of the Mona Lisa, the metadata record would describe the photo and not the Mona Lisa itself.

The Dumb-Down principle stated that the user should be able to look at the information in a metadata field with refinements or qualifications and still be able to make sense of the information if the refinements or qualifications were stripped away. For example, the information contained in a title.alternative field should still make sense to the user if the "alternative" refinement were taken away.

The Appropriate Values principle stated that the metadata producer could never assume that their metadata would only be seen by a certain audience or in a certain context, so metadata should always be produced so that it would be understandable by any user in any context. For example, an early twentieth-century picture of the New Mexico State University Marching Band with the title "The Band" would be perfectly understandable for a user looking at a metadata record with an image on campus or in the nearby area; but someone in Michigan who finds the harvested metadata with no accompanying image may have no idea which band or what is being referred to. Good, harvested metadata needs to stand on its own, independent of context.

Changes to Dublin Core

Since the development of the initial Dublin Core metadata elements, the World Wide Web has grown and changed the way we live, produce, and consume information. Dublin Core has changed as well. Where it was once intended solely for the description of electronic resources created and made available on the web, it is now used for "any object that can be identified, whether electronic, real-world, or conceptual" (Dublin Core Metadata Initiative, 2011a). The simplicity of the original 15 elements led to Dublin Core becoming a common, minimum standard for the transmission of metadata, such as with the Open Archives Initiative Protocol for Metadata Harvesting (OAI-PMH). However, this simplicity became as much of a hindrance for some metadata producers as it was an advantage for others. Over time, additional elements and granularity for the original elements were added to make it a more robust and useful standard for description.

Substantial changes have taken place to Dublin Core over the years. For a long time, the Dublin Core Metadata Element Set (DCMES) was composed only of the 15 initial elements, with the additional elements and refinements being added to the specification under the heading of "Other elements and element refinements" as they were developed. The DCMES came to be known as "Simple Dublin Core," with the DCMES plus additional elements and refinements becoming known as "Qualified Dublin Core." In 2008, the initial and additional elements were combined, redefined as "properties," and joined with guidelines on the use of encoding schemes and controlled vocabularies into one large specification known as the DCMI Metadata Terms. Within the terms, there is still a specification for the DCMES, allowing people to continue using "Simple Dublin Core."

There have also been changes to two of the three principles. The One-to-One principle is largely the same, but the Dumb-Down and Appropriate Values principles have changed and developed in response to technological advances just as Dublin Core has. The Dumb-Down principle has slowly made the move from concentrating on the simplification of metadata to promoting the use of "formal definitions . . . to align metadata description based on different vocabularies" (Dublin Core, 2011b).

The discussion about Appropriate Values has evolved to incorporate ideas on domains and ranges from the Semantic Web, specifically the Resource Description Framework (RDF). More information about RDF is provided in the last chapter in the book. Essentially, domains and ranges provide each of the DCMI properties with more information that can be interpreted by a machine to link data together across the Semantic Web. While this is an important next step for keeping Dublin Core relevant in the changing online environment, for the purposes of this book we'll focus on the DCMI element definitions and uses.

The DCMI Metadata Terms

There are four terms that serve as the building blocks for resource description in Dublin Core. These terms are properties, classes, datatypes, and vocabulary encoding schemes. Together, these building blocks allow a complete and standardized description of a resource. The following definitions come from the DCMI_MediaWiki User Guide (DCMI, 2011a).

Properties – Properties are what used to be called "elements" in Dublin Core. They are the "core attributes of resources" and allow "uniform structured resource description."

Classes – Classes in Dublin Core are ways of grouping resources that have properties in common. In many cases, these classes are defined by the DCMI Type Vocabularies (*http://dublincore.org/documents/dcmi-terms/#H7*), making a class something like a collection, moving image, or physical object.

Datatypes – Datatypes were previously known as Syntax Encoding Schemes (SES). These are rules that govern how the information in certain properties is structured. These rules are used in properties such as dates, type, and format.

Vocabulary Encoding Scheme – Vocabulary Encoding Schemes were previously known as Concept Schemes. They are vocabularies whose terms should be used to structure the information in properties such as creator, contributor, and subject.

Understanding the use of the properties will be the most important part of creating Dublin Core metadata for many professionals in the cultural heritage community. For a simple starting point, this text will begin with the properties in the DCMES, listed below. It will then move on to definitions of the other properties contained in the DCMI Metadata Terms. The definitions come from the DCMES namespace (*http://dublincore.org/documents/dcmi-terms/#H3*) and the DCMI_Media Wiki User Guide for Creating Metadata (*http://wiki.dublincore.org/index.php/User_Guide/Creating_Metadata*).

The DCMES

contributor	format	rights
coverage	identifier	source
creator	language	subject
date	publisher	title
description	relation	type

DCMES Property definitions

contributor

Label: Contributor

Definition: An entity responsible for making contributions to the resource.

Comment: Examples of a contributor include a person, an organization, or a service. Typically, the name of a contributor should be used to indicate the entity. Recommended best practice is to use a controlled vocabulary such as the Library of Congress Name Authority File (LCNAF) or the Getty Union List of Artist Names (ULAN).

coverage

Label: Coverage

Definition: The spatial or temporal topic of the resource, the spatial applicability of the resource, or the jurisdiction under which the resource is relevant.

Comment: Spatial topic and spatial applicability may be a named place or a location specified by its geographic coordinates. Temporal topic may be a named period, date, or date range. A jurisdiction may be a named administrative entity or a geographic place to which the resource applies. Recommended best practice is to use a controlled vocabulary such as the Thesaurus of Geographic Names (TGN). Where appropriate, named places or time periods can be used in preference to numeric identifiers such as sets of coordinates or date ranges.

Former refinements (now DCMI Terms): **spatial** and **temporal.**

creator

Label: Creator

Definition: An entity primarily responsible for making the resource.

Comment: Examples of a creator include a person, an organization, or a service. Typically, the name of the creator should be used to indicate the entity. Recommended best practice is to use a controlled vocabulary such as the LCNAF or the ULAN.

date

Label: Date

Definition: A point or period of time associated with an event in the lifecycle of a resource.

Comment: Date may be used to express temporal information at any level of granularity. Recommended best practice is to use a controlled vocabulary such as ISO 8601.

Former refinements (now DCMI Terms): **created, issued, available, modified, valid, dateCopyrighted, dateSubmitted,** and **dateAccepted.**

description

Label: Description

Definition: An account of the resource.

Comment: Description may include but is not limited to: an abstract, a table of contents, a graphical representation, or a free-text account of the resource.

Former refinements (now DCMI Terms): **abstract, tableOfContents.**

format

Label: Format

Definition: The file format, physical medium or dimensions of the resource.

Comment: Examples of dimension include size and duration. Recommended best practice is to use a controlled vocabulary such as the Internet Media Types (MIME types).

Former refinements (now DCMI Terms): **extent, medium.**

identifier

Label: Identifier

Definition: An unambiguous reference to the resource within a given context.

Comment: Recommended best practice is to identify the resource by means of a string conforming to a formal identification system.

Former refinements (now DCMI Terms): **bibliographicCitation.**

language

Label: Language

Definition: A language of the resource.

Comment: Recommended best practice is to use a controlled vocabulary, such as the three letter language tags of ISO 639.

publisher

Label: Publisher

Definition: An entity responsible for making the resource available.

Comment: Examples of a publisher include a person, an organization, or a service. Typically, the name of a publisher should be used to indicate the entity. Because of the One-to-One principle, the publisher may not be the publisher of a physical object portrayed by a digital object, but the party for making the digital object itself available. Recommended best practice is to use a controlled vocabulary such as the LCNAF when possible.

relation

Label: Relation

Definition: A related resource.

Comment: Recommended best practice is to identify the related resource by means of a string conforming to a formal identification system. Relationships may be described reciprocally, but it is not required.

Former refinements (now DCMI Terms): **isPartOf, hasPart, isVersionOf, hasVersion, isFormatOf, hasFormat, replaces, isReplacedBy, requires, isRequiredBy, references, isReferencedBy, conformsTo.**

rights

Label: Rights

Definition: Information about rights held in and over the resource.

Comment: Typically, rights information includes a statement about various property rights associated with the resource, including intellectual property rights.

Former refinements (now DCMI Terms): **accessRights, license.**

source

Label: Source

Definition: A related resource from which the described resource is derived.

Comment: The described resource may be derived from the related resource in whole or in part. Recommended best practice is to identify the related resource by means of a string conforming to a formal identification system.

subject

Label: Subject

Definition: The topic of the resource.

Comment: Typically, the subject will be represented using keywords, key phrases, or classification codes. Recommended best practice is to use a controlled vocabulary such as LCSH.

title

Label: Title

Definition: A name given to the resource.

Former refinements (now DCMI Terms): **alternative.**

type

Label: Type

Definition: The nature or genre of the resource.

Comment: Recommended best practice is to use a controlled vocabulary such as the DCMI Type Vocabulary (DCMITYPE). To describe the file format, physical medium, or dimensions of the resource, use the **format** element.

Additional DCMI Terms property definitions

abstract

Label: Abstract

Definition: A summary of the resource.

Formerly a refinement of: **description.**

accessRights

Label: Access Rights

Definition: Information about who can access the resource or an indication of its security status.

Comment: Access Rights may include information regarding access or restrictions based on privacy, security, or other policies.

Formerly a refinement of: **rights.**

accrualMethod

Label: Accrual Method

Definition: The method by which items are added to a collection.

accrualPeriodicity

Label: Accrual Periodicity

Definition: The frequency with which items are added to a collection.

accrualPolicy

Label: Accrual Policy

Definition: The policy governing the addition of items to a collection.

alternative

Label: Alternative Title

Definition: An alternative name for the resource.

Comment: The distinction between titles and alternative titles is application-specific.

Formerly a refinement of: **title.**

audience

Label: Audience

Definition: A class of entity for whom the resource is intended or useful.

available

Label: Date Available

Definition: Date (often a range) that the resource became or will become available.

Formerly a refinement of: **date.**

bibliographicCitation

Label: Bibliographic Citation

Definition: A bibliographic reference for the resource.

Comment: Recommended practice is to include sufficient bibliographic detail to identify the resource as unambiguously as possible.

Formerly a refinement of: **identifier.**

conformsTo

Label: Conforms To

Definition: An established standard to which the described resource conforms.

Formerly a refinement of: **relation.**

created

Label: Date Created

Definition: Date of creation of the resource.

Formerly a refinement of: **date.**

dateAccepted

Label: Date Accepted

Definition: Date of acceptance of the resource.

Comment: Examples of resources to which a Date Accepted may be relevant are a thesis (accepted by a university department) or an article (accepted by a journal).

Formerly a refinement of: **date.**

dateCopyrighted

Label: Date Copyrighted

Definition: Date of copyright.

Formerly a refinement of: **date.**

dateSubmitted

Label: Date Submitted

Definition: Date of submission of the resource.

Comment: Examples of resources to which a Date Submitted may be relevant are a thesis (submitted to a university department) or an article (submitted to a journal).

Formerly a refinement of: **date.**

educationLevel

Label: Audience Education Level

Definition: A class of entity, defined in terms of progression through an educational or training context, for which the described resource is intended.

Formerly a refinement of: **audience.**

extent

Label: Extent

Definition: The size or duration of the resource.

Formerly a refinement of: **format.**

hasFormat

Label: Has Format

Definition: A related resource that is substantially the same as the pre-existing described resource, but in another format.

Formerly a refinement of: **relation.**

hasPart

Label: Has Part

Definition: A related resource that is included either physically or logically in the described resource.

Formerly a refinement of: **relation.**

hasVersion

Label: Has Version

Definition: A related resource that is a version, edition, or adaptation of the described resource.

Formerly a refinement of: **relation.**

instructionalMethod

Label: Instructional Method

Definition: A process, used to engender knowledge, attitudes, and skills, that the described resource is designed to support.

Comment: Instructional Method will typically include ways of presenting instructional materials or conducting instructional activities, patterns of learner-to-learner and learner-to-instructor interactions, and mechanisms by which group and individual levels of learning are measured. Instructional methods include all aspects of the instruction and learning processes from planning and implementation through evaluation and feedback.

isFormatOf

Label: Is Format Of

Definition: A related resource that is substantially the same as the described resource, but in another format.

Formerly a refinement of: **relation.**

isPartOf

Label: Is Part Of

Definition: A related resource in which the described resource is physically or logically included.

Formerly a refinement of: **relation.**

isReferencedBy

Label: Is Referenced By

Definition: A related resource that references, cites, or otherwise points to the described resource.

Formerly a refinement of: **relation.**

isReplacedBy

Label: Is Replaced By

Definition: A related resource that supplants, displaces, or supersedes the described resource.

Formerly a refinement of: **relation.**

isRequiredBy

Label: Is Required By

Definition: A related resource that requires the described resource to support its function, delivery, or coherence.

Formerly a refinement of: **relation.**

issued

Label: Date Issued

Definition: Date of formal issuance (e.g. publication) of the resource.

Formerly a refinement of: **date.**

isVersionOf

Label: Is Version Of

Definition: A related resource of which the described resource is a version, edition, or adaptation.

Comment: Changes in version imply substantive changes in content rather than differences in format.

Formerly a refinement of: **relation.**

license

Label: License

Definition: A legal document giving official permission to do something with the resource.

Formerly a refinement of: **rights.**

mediator

Label: Mediator

Definition: An entity that mediates access to the resource and for whom the resource is intended or useful.

Comment: In an educational context, a mediator might be a parent, teacher, teaching assistant, or care-giver.

Formerly a refinement of: **audience.**

medium

Label: Medium

Definition: The material or physical carrier of the resource.

Formerly a refinement of: **format.**

modified

Label: Date Modified

Definition: Date on which the resource was changed.

Formerly a refinement of: **date.**

provenance

Label: Provenance

Definition: A statement of any changes in ownership and custody of the resource since its creation that are significant for its authenticity, integrity, and interpretation.

Comment: The statement may include a description of any changes successive custodians made to the resource.

references

Label: References

Definition: A related resource that is referenced, cited, or otherwise pointed to by the described resource.

Formerly a refinement of: **relation.**

replaces

Label: Replaces

Definition: A related resource that is supplanted, displaced, or superseded by the described resource.

Formerly a refinement of: **relation.**

requires

Label: Requires

Definition: A related resource that is required by the described resource to support its function, delivery, or coherence.

Formerly a refinement of: **relation.**

rightsHolder

Label: Rights Holder

Definition: A person or organization owning or managing rights over the resource.

spatial

Label: Spatial Coverage

Definition: Spatial characteristics of the resource.

Formerly a refinement of: **coverage.**

tableOfContents

Label: Table of Contents

Definition: A list of subunits of the resource.

Formerly a refinement of: **description.**

temporal

Label: Temporal Coverage

Definition: Temporal characteristics of the resource.

Formerly a refinement of: **coverage.**

valid

Label: Date Valid

Definition: Date (often a range) of validity of a resource.

Formerly a refinement of: **date.**

Example record

Figure 3.1 is an example of a Dublin Core metadata record:

Figure 3.1 **NMA&MA Aggies Band**

New Mexico State University Library, Archives and Special Collections

Available information:

Image properties indicate that the digital item was created on February 25, 2009, using Adobe Photoshop CS3 Macintosh, at 8 bits and 300 dpi.

Date created: 2009-02-25

Description: Image shows the NMA&MA Aggies Band, with instruments, on the steps of a building. Digital image was created using Adobe Photoshop CS3 Macintosh, at 8 bits and 300 dpi.

Format: image/jpeg

Identifier: NMA&MA Aggies Band

Is Format Of: NMA&MA Aggies Band

Is Part Of: Hobson-Huntsinger University Archives

Language: eng

Publisher: New Mexico State University Library

Rights: Copyright NMSU Board of Regents

Subject: Marching bands; New Mexico College of Agriculture and Mechanic Arts

Title: New Mexico College of Agriculture and Mechanic Arts Band
Type: Still image

Exercises

The following exercises present digital surrogates of items held by the New Mexico State University Library (Figure 3.2–3.4), along with the information available to the metadata cataloger.

Exercise 3.1

Figure 3.2 **Camel Rock, circa 1948**

New Mexico State University Library, Archives and Special Collections

- Caption on item reads, "Camel Rock near Santa Fe, New Mexico SF-16"
- Date: 31 July 1948 (postmark)
- Digitized on September 3, 2003 using Adobe Photoshop CS3 Macintosh; at 8 bits and 300 dpi
- Notes (in older database): Sold by Old Trail News Agency, Santa Fe, New Mexico Colour Picture Publication, Boston 15, Massachusetts, U.S.A
- Collection: Thomas K. Todsen Photographs

- Collection Number: Ms0223
- Physical description: photocopy and copy negative

Exercise 3.2

Figure 3.3 **Motorcycle Machine Gun Corp, Las Cruces**

New Mexico State University Library, Archives and Special Collections

- Handwritten caption on item reads, "Motorcycle Machine Gun Corps, Las Cruces, 1913"
- Digitized on February 26, 2009 using Adobe Photoshop CS3 Macintosh; at 8 bits and 300 dpi
- Collection: Branigan Memorial Library Photographs
- Collection Number: Ms0001
- Physical item: black and white photograph; located in Ms0001, Box 4, Folder 3; Accession number A76-157/241

Exercise 3.3

Figure 3.4 **Men bagging chili peppers**

New Mexico State University Library, Archives and Special Collections

- Description in older database: Seven men sacking chili peppers for commercial sale
- Digitized on January 13, 2004 using Adobe Photoshop CS5 Macintosh; at 24 bits and 300 dpi
- Date: ca. 1920s-1930s
- Notes: oversize
- Collection: Fabian Garcia Papers
- Collection Number: ua0450
- Physical description: mounted photographic print

Answer key

The production of metadata can sometimes be very subjective, and the fullness of the metadata produced will depend on the amount of information available to the metadata cataloger. However, the following items provide an example of the metadata that could be produced for the above exercises.

Exercise 3.1
Camel Rock, Circa 1948

- Date: 1948?
- Date created: 2003-09-03

- Description: Caption on image reads, "Camel Rock near Santa Fe, New Mexico. SF-16." Image shows Camel Rock, surrounded by bushes. Note in an older database reads, "Sold by Old Trail News Agency, Santa Fe, New Mexico Colour Picture Publication, Boston 15, Massachusetts, U.S.A."
- Format: image/jpeg
- Identifier: 02231280
- Is Format Of: Ms02231280
- Is Part Of: Thomas K. Todsen Photograph Collection, Ms0223
- Language: eng
- Publisher: New Mexico State University Library
- Rights: Copyright NMSU Board of Regents
- Source: photocopy and/or copy negative
- Subject: Camel Rock (N.M.)
- Title: Camel Rock, circa 1948
- Type: Still Image

Exercise 3.2
Motorcycle Machine Gun Corp, Las Cruces

- Date: 1913
- Date Created: 2009-02-26
- Description: Handwritten caption on photograph reads, "Motorcycle Machine Gun Corps, Las Cruces, 1913." Image shows a number of motorcycles parked in a large, grassy area. Digital image was created using Adobe Photoshop CS3 Macintosh, at 8 bits and 300 dpi.
- Format: image/jpeg
- Identifier: Ms00010258
- Is Format Of: Ms00010258
- Is Part Of: Branigan Memorial Library Photographs, Ms0001
- Language: eng
- Publisher: New Mexico State University Library
- Rights: Copyright NMSU Board of Regents
- Source: Ms0001, Box 4, Folder 3: black and white photograph
- Subject: Motorcycle Machine Gun Corp; Machine guns; Motorcycle sidecars

- Title: Motorcycle Machine Gun Corp, Las Cruces
- Type: Still Image

Exercise 3.3
Men bagging chili peppers

- Date: 1920-1930
- Date created: 2004-01-13
- Description: Older database describes the image as, "Seven men sacking chile peppers for commercial sale," and notes that the item is oversized. Digital image was created using Adobe Photoshop CS5 Macintosh, at 24 bits and 300 dpi.
- Format: image/jpeg
- Identifier: 04500241
- Is Format of: ua04500241
- Is Part Of: Fabian Garcia Papers, ua0450
- Publisher: New Mexico State University Library
- Rights: Copyright NMSU Board of Regents
- Source: ua04500241, mounted photographic print
- Subject: Hot peppers; Hot pepper industry
- Title: Men bagging chili peppers
- Type: Still Image

4

Using Encoded Archival Description (EAD)

With information from Encoded Archival Description Tag Library, Version 2002, by the Society of American Archivists

Abstract: This chapter contains brief information on finding aids and their importance to the cultural heritage community, and describes the history and development of the Encoded Archival Description (EAD) metadata language. The chapter provides information on the structural basis of the EAD scheme, definitions for selected individual elements within the scheme, and guidance in the use of the selected elements for metadata creation. The chapter includes an example of an EAD metadata record, exercises allowing the reader to create EAD metadata, and examples of metadata that could be produced for the exercises.

Key words: Metadata, Encoded Archival Description (EAD), Society of American Archivists (SAA), Library of Congress Network Development and MARC Standards Office, Describing Archives: A Content Standard (DACS), finding aids, archival collections.

Introduction

Encoded Archival Description (EAD) is the metadata standard the archives community uses to describe its collections. Archivists collect many different types of materials from individuals, groups, institutions, etc., and keep materials that are acquired from the same place together as a collection. A common type of collection is a collection of personal papers. These papers are separated into file folders, and the folders are placed in boxes. Other types of materials that may be found in archival collections include photographs, maps, scrapbooks, diaries, and newspaper clippings. In order for a user to find materials, these collections must be indexed, and information about the papers in each folder and box must be created. This information is called a finding aid. Finding aids also often include brief biographical or background information about the collection.

Archivists have been creating finding aids for many years. Originally, these finding aids were kept on paper at the archives, and users came in and looked through the finding aid. Each archive had a different way of creating finding aids, and, since there was no way to share them, it didn't matter if Archive A was following different best practices from Archive B. Early computerized finding aids were simple text files, which were difficult to navigate.

However, with the advent of the computer, internet, and associated methods for encoding and sharing, like XML, the archives community decided that it was time to standardize and share finding aids. As soon as encoding standards became common, archives started forming consortia and sharing their finding aids across a shared catalog. Examples of this type of portal are the Rocky Mountain Online Archive (*http://rmoa.unm.edu*), TARO (Texas Archival Resources Online) (*http://www.lib.utexas.edu/taro/index.html*), and OAC (Online Archive of California) (*http://www.oac.cdlib.org*). Because each archive may only have several hundred collections (as opposed to digital libraries with thousands of items), these shared catalogues help minimize cost and maximize exposure for each record.

EAD supports a multilevel description of each collection. The top level is an overview of the entire collection. Types of materials, provenance and access, biographical sketches, and scope and content notes are included at this level. The second level is groupings of materials within the collection. This can include series or subseries, and this level of description is only necessary with very large or complex collections. At the third level of description, each file or item is described. This includes boxes and folders, and a list of items in each container is included.

EAD is defined by an XML document type definition (DTD). DTDs define the structure of an XML document and list the elements and attributes that can be found in the document. In general, XML schemas have replaced DTDs, and the Society of American Archivists has released an EAD 2002 schema, but the DTD is still more commonly used with EAD documents.

Development

EAD began with a project at the University of California, Berkeley, in 1993. At that time, the project developers wanted to create a flexible encoding standard that could accommodate various descriptive practices in libraries, archives, and museums. They recognized that they needed elements beyond what was provided in MARC. The original requirements for EAD included the following criteria:

- ability to present extensive and interrelated descriptive information found in archival finding aids
- ability to preserve the hierarchical relationships existing between levels of description
- ability to represent descriptive information that is inherited by one hierarchical level from another
- ability to move within a hierarchical information structure
- support for element-specific indexing and retrieval. (Library of Congress, 2006)

SGML was chosen as the markup language for the encoding standard due to its ability to establish relationships among parts of the document, and SGML's increasing popularity and use. In 1995, the Society of American Archivists formed an EAD Working Group, and this group accepted responsibility for supporting the development of the EAD DTD, tag library, and application guidelines. The Library of Congress Network Development and MARC Standards office became the official maintenance agency for EAD in 1996. In 2002, the standard was revised and updated, and the DTD was updated to be compatible with XML (a subset of SGML).

EAD is a structure standard. Structure standards define the elements to be used, but do not prescribe how the information should be recorded within the element. Content standards are the rules that define how the information is recorded, and the content standard used most often with EAD is DACS. However, DACS is not specific to EAD, and can also be used with MARC, although the most common content standard used with MARC is AACR2.

As of late 2012, revisions to EAD are under development, with a release date of August 2013.

As with all XML metadata schemas, XSLT can be used to turn the record into an HTML display record.

Elements

The EAD tag set has 146 elements. A PDF of the tag library, with definitions of all elements, can be downloaded from the Library of Congress (*http://www.loc.gov/ead/tglib/index.html*) or the Society of American Archivists (*http://www2.archivists.org/sites/all/files/EAD2002TL_5-03-V2.pdf*).

Below is a list of some basic elements and their definitions from the EAD Tag Library, along with their placement within the EAD hierarchy. Definitions are taken directly from the *Encoded Archival Description Tag Library* available at the Society of American Archivists' website. This is a selected list of EAD elements; not all of the elements are included.

Structural Model

<ead> The outermost wrapper element for an information access tool known generically as a finding aid. A finding aid establishes physical and intellectual control over many types of archival materials and helps researchers understand and access the materials being described. The <ead> element defines a particular instance of a document encoded with the EAD DTD. It contains a required <eadheader>, optional <frontmatter>, and a required <archdesc> element, in that order.

<ead> **<eadheader>** A wrapper element for bibliographic and descriptive information about the finding aid document rather than the archival materials being described. The <eadheader> is modeled on the Text Encoding Initiative (TEI) header element to encourage uniformity in the provision of metadata across document types.

<ead> <eadheader> **<eadid>** A required subelement of <eadheader> that designates a unique code for a particular EAD finding aid document.

<ead> <eadheader> **<filedesc>** A required subelement of the <eadheader> that bundles much of the bibliographic information about the finding aid, including its author, title, subtitle, and sponsor (all in the <titlestmt>), as well as the edition, publisher, publishing series, and related notes (encoded separately).

<ead> <eadheader> **<profiledesc>** An optional subelement of the <eadheader> that bundles information about the creation of the encoded version of the finding aid, including the name of the agent, place, and date of encoding. The <profiledesc> element also designates the predominant and minor languages used in the finding aid.

<ead> <eadheader> **<revisiondesc>** An optional subelement of the <eadheader> for information about changes or alterations that have been made to the encoded finding aid. The revisions may be recorded as part of a <list> or as a series of <change> elements. Like much of the <eadheader>, the <revisiondesc> element is modeled on an element found in the TEI DTD. The TEI recommends that revisions be numbered and appear in reverse chronological order, with the most recent <change> first.

<ead> **<frontmatter>** A wrapper element that bundles prefatory text found before the start of the Archival Description <archdesc>. It focuses on the creation, publication, or use of the finding aid rather than information about the materials being described. Examples include a title page, preface, dedication, and instructions for using a finding aid. The optional <titlepage> element within <frontmatter> can be used to repeat selected information from the <eadheader> to generate a title page that follows local preferences for sequencing information. The other <frontmatter> structures, such as a dedication, are encoded as Text Divisions <div>s, with a <head> element containing word(s) that identify the nature of the text.

<ead> **<archdesc>** A wrapper element for the bulk of an EAD document instance, which describes the content, context, and extent of a body of archival materials, including administrative and supplemental information that facilitates use of the materials. Information is organized in unfolding, hierarchical levels that allow a descriptive overview of the whole to be followed by more detailed views of the parts, designated by the element Description of Subordinate Components <dsc>. Data elements available at the <archdesc> level are repeated at the various component levels within <dsc>, and information is inherited from one hierarchical level to the next.

<ead> <archdesc> **<did>** A required wrapper element that bundles other elements identifying core information about the described materials in either Archival Description <archdesc> or a Component <c>. The various <did> subelements are intended for brief, clearly designated statements of information and, except for <note>, do not require Paragraphs <p> to enter text.

The <did> groups elements that constitute a good basic description of an archival unit. This grouping ensures that the same data elements and structure are available at every level of description within the EAD hierarchy. It facilitates the retrieval or other output of a cohesive body of elements for resource discovery and recognition.

<ead> <archdesc> <did> **<repository>** The institution or agency responsible for providing intellectual access to the materials being described. The <corpname> element may be used within <repository> to encode the institution's proper name.

<ead> <archdesc> <did> **<origination>** Information about the individual or organization responsible for the creation, accumulation, or assembly of the described materials before their incorporation into an archival repository. The <origination> element may be used to indicate such agents as correspondents, records creators, collectors, and dealers. Using the LABEL attribute may help identify for a finding aid reader the role of the originator, e.g., "creator," "collector," or "photographer." It is also possible to set the ROLE attribute on the name elements that are available within <origination>, i.e. <corpname>, <famname>, <name>, and <persname>.

<ead> <archdesc> <did> **<unittitle>** The name, either formal or supplied, of the described materials. May consist of a word, phrase, character, or group of characters. As an important subelement of the Descriptive Identification <did>, the <unittitle> encodes the name of the described materials at both the highest unit or <archdesc> level (e.g. collection, record group, or fonds) and at all the subordinate Component <c> levels (e.g. subseries, files, items, or other intervening stages within a hierarchical description).

<ead> <archdesc> <did> **<unitdate>** The creation year, month, or day of the described materials. The <unitdate> may be in the form of text or numbers, and may consist of a single date or range of dates. As an important subelement of the Descriptive Identification <did>, the <unitdate> is used to tag only the creation and other relevant dates of the materials described in the encoded finding aid. Do not confuse it with the <date> element, which is used to tag all other dates.

<ead> <archdesc> <did> **<physdesc>** A wrapper element for bundling information about the appearance or construction of the described materials, such as their dimensions, a count of their quantity or statement about the space they occupy, and terms describing their genre, form, or function, as well as any other aspects of their appearance, such as color, substance, style, and technique or method of creation. The information may be presented as plain text, or it may be divided into the <dimension>, <extent>, <genreform>, and <physfacet> subelements.

<ead> <archdesc> <did> **<unitid>** Any alpha-numeric text string that serves as a unique reference point or control number for the described material, such as a lot number, an accession number, a classification number, or an entry number in a bibliography or catalog. An important subelement of the Descriptive Identification <did>, the <unitid> is primarily a logical designation, which sometimes secondarily provides location information, as in the case of a classification number. Use other <did> subelements, such as <physloc> and <container>, to designate specifically the physical location of the described materials.

<ead> <archdesc> <did> **<abstract>** A very brief summary of the materials being described, used primarily to encode bits of biographical or historical information about the creator and abridged statements about the scope, content, arrangement, or other descriptive details about the archival unit or one of its components.

<ead> <archdesc> <did> **<langmaterial>** A prose statement enumerating the language(s) of the archival materials found in the unit being described.

<ead> <archdesc> <did> **<materialspec>** Data which are unique to a particular class or form of material and which are not assigned to any other element of description. Examples of material specific details include mathematical data, such as scale for cartographic and architectural records, jurisdictional and denominational data for philatelic records, and physical presentation data for music records.

<ead> <archdesc> <did> **<physloc>** Information identifying the place where the described materials are stored, such as the name or number of the building, room, stack, shelf, or other tangible area.

<ead> <archdesc> <did> **<container>** A <did> subelement for information that contributes to locating the described materials by indicating the kinds of devices that hold the materials and identifying any sequential numbers assigned to those devices. The <container> element is used most frequently at the component level, i.e. once a Description of Subordinate Components <dsc> has been opened. This storage information can help researchers understand how extensive the material is, especially in the absence of a specific physical <extent> statement at the component level.

<ead> <archdesc> <did> **<note>** A generic element that provides a short statement explaining the text, indicating the basis for an assertion, or citing the source of a quotation or other information. Used both

for general comments and as an annotation for the text in a finding aid. Not used when more specific content designation elements are appropriate, e.g. <abstract>, <altformavail>, <archref>, or <scopecontent>. Do not confuse with Other Descriptive Data <odd> element, which is used within <archdesc> and <c> to designate information that is more than a short comment in a <note>.

<ead> <archdesc> <did> **<dao>** A linking element that uses the attributes ENTITYREF or HREF to connect the finding aid information to electronic representations of the described materials. The <dao> and <daogrp> elements allow the content of an archival collection or record group to be incorporated in the finding aid. These digital representations include graphic images, audio or video clips, images of text pages, and electronic transcriptions of text. The objects can be selected examples, or digital surrogates of all the materials in an archival fonds or series. / <daogrp> A wrapper element that contains two or more related Digital Archival Object Locations <daoloc> that should be thought of as a group and may share a single common Digital Archival Object Description <daodesc>. They may also form an extended link group to enable a set of multidirectional links. The <dao>, <daogrp>, and <daoloc> elements allow the content of the described materials to be incorporated in the finding aid.

<ead> <archdesc> **<descgrp>** An element that can be used to bring together any group of elements that are children of the Archival Description <archdesc> element except for the <did> and <dsc> elements. Description Group might be used, for example, to cluster elements into groups that correspond to the areas specified by the General International Standard Archival Description (ISAD(G)).

<ead> <archdesc> **<bioghist>** A concise essay or chronology that places the archival materials in context by providing information about their creator(s). Includes significant information about the life of an individual or family, or the administrative history of a corporate body. The <bioghist> may contain just text in a series of Paragraphs <p>, and/or a Chronology List <chronlist> that matches dates and date ranges with associated events. Additional <bioghist> elements may be nested inside one another when a complex body of materials, such as a collection of family papers, is being described, and separately headed sections are desired. The <bioghist> element may also be nested to designate a portion of the essay or chronology that might be extracted as a MARC 545 subfield.

<ead> <archdesc> **<scopecontent>** A prose statement summarizing the range and topical coverage of the described materials, often mentioning the form and arrangement of the materials and naming significant organizations, individuals, events, places, and subjects represented. The purpose of the <scopecontent> element is to assist readers in evaluating the potential relevance of the materials to their research. It may highlight particular strengths of, or gaps in, the described materials and may summarize in narrative form some of the descriptive information entered in other parts of the finding aid.

<ead> <archdesc> **<arrangement>** Information on how the described materials have been subdivided into smaller units, e.g. record groups into series, identifying the logical or physical groupings within a hierarchical structure. Can also be used to express the filing sequence of the described materials, such as the principal characteristics of the internal structure, or the physical or logical ordering of materials, including alphabetical, chronological, geographical, office of origin, and other schemes. Identifying logical groupings and the arrangement pattern may enhance retrieval by researchers.

<ead> <archdesc> **<accessrestrict>** Information about conditions that affect the availability of the materials being described. May indicate the need for an appointment or the nature of restrictions imposed by the donor, legal statute, repository, or other agency. May also indicate the lack of restrictions.

<ead> <archdesc> **<userestrict>** Information about conditions that affect use of the described materials after access has been granted. May indicate limitations, regulations, or special procedures imposed by a repository, donor, legal statute, or other agency regarding reproduction, publication, or quotation of the described materials. May also indicate the absence of restrictions, such as when copyright or literary rights have been dedicated to the public. Do not confuse with Conditions Governing Access <accessrestrict>, which designates information about conditions affecting the availability of the described materials. Preferred Citation <prefercite> may be used in conjunction with <userestrict> to encode statements specifying how the described materials should be referenced when reproduced, published, or quoted by patrons.

<ead> <archdesc> **<custodhist>** Information about the chain of ownership of the materials being described, before they reached the immediate source of acquisition. Both physical possession and intellectual ownership can be described, providing details of changes of

ownership and/or custody that may be significant in terms of authority, integrity, and interpretation.

<ead> <archdesc> **<altformavail>** Information about copies of the materials being described, including the type of alternative form, significant control numbers, location, and source for ordering if applicable. The additional formats are typically microforms, photocopies, or digital reproductions.

<ead> <archdesc> **<originalsloc>** Information about the existence, location, availability, and/or the destruction of originals where the unit described consists of copies.

<ead> <archdesc> **<phystech>** A description of important physical conditions or characteristics that affect the storage, preservation, or use of the materials described. This includes details of their physical composition or the need for particular hardware or software to preserve or access the materials.

<ead> <archdesc> **<prefercite>** Information about how users should identify the described materials when referring to them in published credits. Generally the repository or agent responsible for providing intellectual access to the materials will supply users with a recommended wording or prescribed format for structuring references to the described materials in bibliographies, footnotes, screen credits, etc.

<ead> <archdesc> **<acqinfo>** The immediate source of the materials being described and the circumstances under which they were received. Includes donations, transfers, purchases, and deposits.

<ead> <archdesc> **<accruals>** Information about anticipated additions to the materials being described. Can indicate quantity and frequency. Can also be used to indicate that no additions are expected.

<ead> <archdesc> **<appraisal>** Information about the process of determining the archival value and thus the disposition of records based upon their current administrative, legal, and fiscal use; their evidential, intrinsic, and informational value; their arrangement and condition; and their relationship to other records.

<ead> <archdesc> **<processinfo>** Information about accessioning, arranging, describing, preserving, storing, or otherwise preparing the described materials for research use. Specific aspects of each of these activities may be encoded separately within other elements, such as <acqinfo>, <arrangement>, <physloc>, etc.

<ead> <archdesc> **<controlaccess>** A wrapper element that designates key access points for the described materials and enables authority-controlled searching across finding aids on a computer network. Hundreds of names and subjects can appear in a finding aid. Prominence can be given to the major ones by bundling them together in a single place within the <archdesc> or within a large Component <c> and tagging them with <controlaccess>.

<ead> <archdesc> <controlaccess> **<corpname>** The proper noun name that identifies an organization or group of people that acts as an entity. Examples include names of associations, institutions, business firms, nonprofit enterprises, governments, government agencies, projects, programs, religious bodies, churches, conferences, athletic contests, exhibitions, expeditions, fairs, and ships.

<ead> <archdesc> <controlaccess> **<famname>** The proper noun designation for a group of persons closely related by blood or persons who form a household. Includes single families and family groups, e.g. Patience Parker Family and Parker Family.

<ead> <archdesc> <controlaccess> **<genreform>** A term that identifies the types of material being described, by naming the style or technique of their intellectual content (genre); order of information or object function (form); and physical characteristics. Examples include: account books, architectural drawings, portraits, short stories, sound recordings, and videotapes.

<ead> <archdesc> <controlaccess> **<geogname>** The proper noun designation for a place, natural feature, or political jurisdiction. Examples include: Appalachian Mountains; Baltimore, Md.; Chinatown, San Francisco; and Kew Gardens, England.

<ead> <archdesc> <controlaccess> **<occupation>** A term identifying a type of work, profession, trade, business, or avocation significantly reflected in the materials being described.

<ead> <archdesc> <controlaccess> **<persname>** The proper noun designation for an individual, including any or all of that individual's forenames, surnames, honorific titles, and added names.

<ead> <archdesc> <controlaccess> **<subject>** A term that identifies a topic associated with or covered by the described materials. Personal, corporate, and geographic names behaving as subjects are tagged as <persname>, <corpname>, and <geogname>, respectively. The ROLE attribute can be set to "subject" when it is necessary to specify the relationship of the name to the materials being described.

<ead> <archdesc> **<odd>** An element for information about the described materials that is not easily incorporated into one of the other named elements within <archdesc> and <c>. When converting finding aids to an ideal EAD markup, some shifting of text or addition of data may be necessary to conform to the DTD's sequencing of elements and the consignment of certain elements to specific settings. The <odd> element helps to minimize conversion difficulties by designating, as "other," information that does not fit easily into one of EAD's more distinct categories.

<ead> <archdesc> **<bibliography>** Citations to works that are based on, about, or of special value when using the materials being described, or works in which a citation to or brief description of the materials is available. The works could be books, articles, television programs, unpublished reports, websites, or other forms of information. The <bibliography> may be a simple <list>, a list of both Bibliographic References <bibref> and Archival References <archref>, or a series of Paragraphs <p>.

<ead> <archdesc> **<fileplan>** Information about any classification scheme used for arranging, storing, and retrieving the described materials by the parties originally responsible for creating or compiling them. A filing plan is usually identified by the type of system used, e.g. alphabetical, numerical, alpha-numerical, decimal, color-coded, etc. It is often hierarchical and may include the filing guidelines of the originating organization. Additional types include a drawing of a room layout or a scientific scheme.

<ead> <archdesc> **<index>** A list of key terms and reference pointers that have been assembled to enhance access to the materials being described. The <index> can also serve as a helpful alphabetical overview of subjects, correspondents, photographers, or other entities represented in the collection. This back-of-the-volume <index> may provide hypertext links, or it may note the container numbers useful for locating the position in the finding aid where the indexed material appears.

<ead> <archdesc> **<otherfindaid>** Information about additional or alternative guides to the described material, such as card files, dealers' inventories, or lists generated by the creator or compiler of the materials. It is used to indicate the existence of additional finding aids; it is not designed to encode the content of those guides.

<ead> <archdesc> **<relatedmaterial>** Information about materials that are not physically or logically included in the material described in

the finding aid but that may be of use to a reader because of an association to the described materials. Materials designated by this element are not related to the described material by provenance, accumulation, or use.

<ead> <archdesc> **<separatedmaterial>** Information about materials that are associated by provenance to the described materials but that have been physically separated or removed. Items may be separated for various reasons, including the dispersal of special formats to more appropriate custodial units; the outright destruction of duplicate or nonessential material; and the deliberate or unintentional scattering of fonds among different repositories. Do not confuse with <relatedmaterial>, which is used to encode descriptions of or references to materials that are not physically or logically included in the material described in the finding aid but that may be of use to a reader because of an association to the described materials. Items encoded as <relatedmaterial> are not related to the described material by provenance, accumulation, or use.

<ead> <archdesc> **<dsc>** (Description of subordinate components) A wrapper element that bundles information about the hierarchical groupings of the materials being described. The subordinate components can be presented in several different forms or levels of descriptive detail, which are identified by the element's required TYPE attribute. For example, "analyticover" identifies an overview description of series and subseries, which might be followed by a second <dsc> with the TYPE attribute set to "in-depth" that provides a more detailed listing of the content of the materials, including information about the container numbers associated with those materials. The TYPE attribute value "combined" is used when the description of a series is followed immediately by a listing of the contents of that series. The TYPE attribute "othertype" is for models that do not follow any of the above-mentioned formats, in which case the OTHERTYPE attribute can then be used to specify a particular presentation model.

<ead> <archdesc> <dsc> **<c01>** A wrapper element that designates the top or first-level subordinate part of the materials being described. Components may be either unnumbered <c> or numbered <c01>, <c02>, etc. The numbered components <c01> to <c12> assist a finding aid encoder in nesting up to 12 component levels accurately.

<ead> <archdesc> <dsc> <c01> **<did>** A required wrapper element that bundles other elements identifying core information about the

described materials in either Archival Description <archdesc> or a Component <c>. The various <did> subelements are intended for brief, clearly designated statements of information and, except for <note>, do not require Paragraphs <p> to enter text.

<ead> <archdesc> <dsc> <c01> **<descgrp>** An element that can be used to bring together any group of elements that are children of the Archival Description <archdesc> element except for the <did> and <dsc> elements. Description Group might be used, for example, to cluster elements into groups that correspond to the areas specified by the General International Standard Archival Description (ISAD(G)).

<ead> <archdesc> <dsc> <c01> **<bioghist>** A concise essay or chronology that places the archival materials in context by providing information about their creator(s). Includes significant information about the life of an individual or family, or the administrative history of a corporate body. The <bioghist> may contain just text in a series of Paragraphs <p>, and/or a Chronology List <chronlist> that matches dates and date ranges with associated events. Additional <bioghist> elements may be nested inside one another when a complex body of materials, such as a collection of family papers, is being described, and separately headed sections are desired. The <bioghist> element may also be nested to designate a portion of the essay or chronology that might be extracted as a MARC 545 subfield.

<ead> <archdesc> <dsc> <c01> **<scopecontent>** A prose statement summarizing the range and topical coverage of the described materials, often mentioning the form and arrangement of the materials and naming significant organizations, individuals, events, places, and subjects represented. The purpose of the <scopecontent> element is to assist readers in evaluating the potential relevance of the materials to their research. It may highlight particular strengths of, or gaps in, the described materials and may summarize in narrative form some of the descriptive information entered in other parts of the finding aid.

<ead> <archdesc> <dsc> <c01> **<arrangement>** Information on how the described materials have been subdivided into smaller units, e.g. record groups into series, identifying the logical or physical groupings within a hierarchical structure. Can also be used to express the filing sequence of the described materials, such as the principal characteristics of the internal structure, or the physical or logical ordering of materials, including alphabetical, chronological, geographical, office of origin, and other schemes. Identifying logical

groupings and the arrangement pattern may enhance retrieval by researchers.

<ead> <archdesc> <dsc> <c01> **<accessrestrict>** Information about conditions that affect the availability of the materials being described. May indicate the need for an appointment or the nature of restrictions imposed by the donor, legal statute, repository, or other agency. May also indicate the lack of restrictions.

<ead> <archdesc> <dsc> <c01> **<userestrict>** Information about conditions that affect use of the described materials after access has been granted. May indicate limitations, regulations, or special procedures imposed by a repository, donor, legal statute, or other agency regarding reproduction, publication, or quotation of the described materials. May also indicate the absence of restrictions, such as when copyright or literary rights have been dedicated to the public. Do not confuse with Conditions Governing Access <accessrestrict>, which designates information about conditions affecting the availability of the described materials. Preferred Citation <prefercite> may be used in conjunction with <userestrict> to encode statements specifying how the described materials should be referenced when reproduced, published, or quoted by patrons.

<ead> <archdesc> <dsc> <c01> **<custodhist>** Information about the chain of ownership of the materials being described, before they reached the immediate source of acquisition. Both physical possession and intellectual ownership can be described, providing details of changes of ownership and/or custody that may be significant in terms of authority, integrity, and interpretation.

<ead> <archdesc> <dsc> <c01> **<altformavail>** Information about copies of the materials being described, including the type of alternative form, significant control numbers, location, and source for ordering if applicable. The additional formats are typically microforms, photocopies, or digital reproductions.

<ead> <archdesc> <dsc> <c01> **<originalsloc>** Information about the existence, location, availability, and/or the destruction of originals where the unit described consists of copies.

<ead> <archdesc> <dsc> <c01> **<phystech>** A description of important physical conditions or characteristics that affect the storage, preservation, or use of the materials described. This includes details of their physical composition or the need for particular hardware or software to preserve or access the materials.

<ead> <archdesc> <dsc> <c01> **<prefercite>** Information about how users should identify the described materials when referring to them in published credits. Generally the repository or agent responsible for providing intellectual access to the materials will supply users with a recommended wording or prescribed format for structuring references to the described materials in bibliographies, footnotes, screen credits, etc.

<ead> <archdesc> <dsc> <c01> **<acqinfo>** The immediate source of the materials being described and the circumstances under which they were received. Includes donations, transfers, purchases, and deposits.

<ead> <archdesc> <dsc> <c01> **<accruals>** Information about anticipated additions to the materials being described. Can indicate quantity and frequency. Can also be used to indicate that no additions are expected.

<ead> <archdesc> <dsc> <c01> **<appraisal>** Information about the process of determining the archival value and thus the disposition of records based upon their current administrative, legal, and fiscal use; their evidential, intrinsic, and informational value; their arrangement and condition; and their relationship to other records.

<ead> <archdesc> <dsc> <c01> **<processinfo>** Information about accessioning, arranging, describing, preserving, storing, or otherwise preparing the described materials for research use. Specific aspects of each of these activities may be encoded separately within other elements, such as <acqinfo>, <arrangement>, <physloc>, etc.

<ead> <archdesc> <dsc> <c01> **<controlaccess>** A wrapper element that designates key access points for the described materials and enables authority-controlled searching across finding aids on a computer network. Hundreds of names and subjects can appear in a finding aid. Prominence can be given to the major ones by bundling them together in a single place within the <archdesc> or within a large Component <c> and tagging them with <controlaccess>.

<ead> <archdesc> <dsc> <c01> **<odd>** (Other Descriptive Data) An element for information about the described materials that is not easily incorporated into one of the other named elements within <archdesc> and <c>. When converting finding aids to an ideal EAD markup, some shifting of text or addition of data may be necessary to conform to the DTD's sequencing of elements and the consignment of certain elements to specific settings. The <odd> element helps to minimize conversion difficulties by designating, as "other,"

information that does not fit easily into one of EAD's more distinct categories.

<ead> <archdesc> <dsc> <c01> **<bibliography>** Citations to works that are based on, about, or of special value when using the materials being described, or works in which a citation to or brief description of the materials is available. The works could be books, articles, television programs, unpublished reports, websites, or other forms of information. The <bibliography> may be a simple <list>, a list of both Bibliographic References <bibref> and Archival References <archref>, or a series of Paragraphs <p>.

<ead> <archdesc> <dsc> <c01> **<fileplan>** Information about any classification scheme used for arranging, storing, and retrieving the described materials by the parties originally responsible for creating or compiling them. A filing plan is usually identified by the type of system used, e.g. alphabetical, numerical, alpha-numerical, decimal, color-coded, etc. It is often hierarchical and may include the filing guidelines of the originating organization. Additional types include a drawing of a room layout or a scientific scheme.

<ead> <archdesc> <dsc> <c01> **<index>** A list of key terms and reference pointers that have been assembled to enhance access to the materials being described. The <index> can also serve as a helpful alphabetical overview of subjects, correspondents, photographers, or other entities represented in the collection. This back-of-the-volume <index> may provide hypertext links, or it may note the container numbers useful for locating the position in the finding aid where the indexed material appears.

<ead> <archdesc> <dsc> <c01> **<otherfindaid>** Information about additional or alternative guides to the described material, such as card files, dealers' inventories, or lists generated by the creator or compiler of the materials. It is used to indicate the existence of additional finding aids; it is not designed to encode the content of those guides.

<ead> <archdesc> <dsc> <c01> **<relatedmaterial>** Information about materials that are not physically or logically included in the material described in the finding aid but that may be of use to a reader because of an association to the described materials. Materials designated by this element are not related to the described material by provenance, accumulation, or use.

<ead> <archdesc> <dsc> <c01> **<separatedmaterial>** Information about materials that are associated by provenance to the described materials

but that have been physically separated or removed. Items may be separated for various reasons, including the dispersal of special formats to more appropriate custodial units; the outright destruction of duplicate or nonessential material; and the deliberate or unintentional scattering of fonds among different repositories. Do not confuse with <relatedmaterial>, which is used to encode descriptions of or references to materials that are not physically or logically included in the material described in the finding aid but that may be of use to a reader because of an association to the described materials. Items encoded as <relatedmaterial> are not related to the described material by provenance, accumulation, or use.

<ead> <archdesc> <dsc> <c01> **<c02>** A wrapper element that designates a second-level subordinate part of the materials being described. Components may be either unnumbered <c> or numbered <c01>, <c02>, etc. The numbered components <c01> to <c12> assist a finding aid encoder in nesting up to 12 component levels accurately.

<ead> <archdesc> <dsc> <c01> <c02> **<did>** (Descriptive Identification) A required wrapper element that bundles other elements identifying core information about the described materials in either Archival Description <archdesc> or a Component <c>. The various <did> subelements are intended for brief, clearly designated statements of information and, except for <note>, do not require Paragraphs <p> to enter text.

<ead> <archdesc> <dsc> <c01> <c02> **<bioghist>** (Biography or History) A concise essay or chronology that places the archival materials in context by providing information about their creator(s). Includes significant information about the life of an individual or family, or the administrative history of a corporate body. The <bioghist> may contain just text in a series of Paragraphs <p>, and/or a Chronology List <chronlist> that matches dates and date ranges with associated events. Additional <bioghist> elements may be nested inside one another when a complex body of materials, such as a collection of family papers, is being described, and separately headed sections are desired. The <bioghist> element may also be nested to designate a portion of the essay or chronology that might be extracted as a MARC 545 subfield.

<ead> <archdesc> <dsc> <c01> <c02> **<scopecontent>** A prose statement summarizing the range and topical coverage of the described materials, often mentioning the form and arrangement of the materials and naming significant organizations, individuals, events, places, and subjects represented. The purpose of the <scopecontent>

element is to assist readers in evaluating the potential relevance of the materials to their research. It may highlight particular strengths of, or gaps in, the described materials and may summarize in narrative form some of the descriptive information entered in other parts of the finding aid.

<ead> <archdesc> <dsc> <c01> <c02> <c03> etc.

In addition to the structural elements listed, the <did>-level elements also contain heads and paragraph elements (<head> and <p>) as well as other textual formatting elements.

Example EAD record (abbreviated)

The following record is an abbreviated record from the Rocky Mountain Online Archive. Full item descriptions and subject analysis have been removed from this record. See *http://rmoa.unm.edu/docviewer.php?docId=nmupict2000-017.xml* for the complete record.

```
<ead>
  <eadheader findaidstatus="edited-full-draft"
langencoding="iso639-2b" audience="internal"
repositoryencoding="iso15511" countryencoding="iso3166-1"
scriptencoding="iso15924" dateencoding="iso8601"
relatedencoding="Dublin Core">
    <eadid publicid="-//University of New Mexico Center
for Southwest Research//TEXT(US::NmU::PICT 2000-017)//EN"
countrycode="us" mainagencycode="NmU"
encodinganalog="Identifier"/>
    <filedesc>
      <titlestmt>
        <titleproper encodinganalog="Title">Inventory
of the Lee Marmon Pictorial Collection,
<date>1936–2010</date></titleproper>
      </titlestmt>
      <publicationstmt>
        <publisher>University of New Mexico,
University Libraries, Center for Southwest
Research</publisher>
          <date era="ce" calendar="gregorian"
encodinganalog="Date">© 2007</date>
```

```
          <p>The University of New Mexico</p>
     </publicationstmt>
   </filedesc>
   <profiledesc>
     <langusage>Finding aid is in <language
encodinganalog="Language" langcode="eng">English
</language></langusage>
   </profiledesc>
  </eadheader>
  <archdesc level="collection" relatedencoding="MARC 21">
   <did>
     <head>Collection Summary</head>
     <unittitle encodinganalog="245" label="Title">Lee
Marmon Pictorial Collection</unittitle>
     <unitdate type="inclusive" era="ce"
calendar="gregorian" normal="1936/2008">1936-2010
</unitdate>
     <unitid countrycode="us" label="Collection
Number">PICT 2000-017</unitid>
     <origination label="Creator">
       <persname>Marmon, Lee</persname>
     </origination>
     <physdesc encodinganalog="300" label="Size">
       <extent>36 boxes</extent>
     </physdesc>
     <physloc>B2. Filed by Accession Number.</physloc>
     <repository encodinganalog="852"
label="Repository">
       <corpname>University of New Mexico Center for
Southwest Research</corpname>
     </repository>
     <abstract>This collection contains photographs taken
by Lee Marmon throughout his life. These include images
of elders and community members from Laguna and Acoma
Pueblos, visual documentation of uranium mines and mills
throughout New Mexico, photos of fashion and social life
in 1960s and 1970s Palm Springs, CA, among other
things.</abstract>
   </did>
   <arrangement>
     <head>Arrangement of the Collection:</head>
```

```
     <p>The Lee Marmon Pictorial Collection is arranged
into series: </p>
     <list type="marked">
       <item>Original Lee Marmon Collection (2000)</item>
       <item> American Indian Colleges </item>
       <item>General Photographs</item>
       <item>Moving Images</item>
     </list>
   </arrangement>
   <dsc type="in-depth">
     <head>Contents List</head>
     <c01 level="series">
       <did>
         <unittitle id="orig">ORIGINAL MARMON COLLECTION
(2000)</unittitle>
         <unitdate>1949-1999</unitdate>
       </did>
       <c02 level="file">
         <did>
           <container type="box">1</container>
           <container type="folder">1</container>
           <unittitle>Portraits - Men </unittitle>
           <unitdate>1949–1963</unitdate>
         </did>
         <scopecontent><p>0001:Lee Marmon with Station
Wagon,1949. 0002: Jeff Sousea "White Man's
Moccasins,"1954. 0003: Gov. James Solomon w/ Lincoln
cane, 1958. 0004: Mateos Mexicano, 1962; 0005: Jose
Sanshu, 1963; 0006: Jose Teofilo, 1961; 0007: Fernando,
1950; 0008: John Riley, 1949</p></scopecontent>
       </c02>
       <c02 level="file">
         <did>
           <container type="box">2</container>
           <container type="folder">1</container>
           <unittitle>Portraits - Men and Women</unittitle>
           <unitdate>1952-1987</unitdate>
         </did>
         <scopecontent><p>0009: Benson, Navajo
Sheepherder, 1985; 0010: Bronco Martinez,1984; 0011:
Platero, Navajo, 1962; 0012: Bennie, 1984; 0013: Fr.
```

```
Kenneth, Acoma, 1952; 0014: Esther – Zuni Pueblo, 1975;
0015: Susie Rayos Marmon, 110th birthday, 1987; 0016:
Lucy Louis - Acoma, 1960</p></scopecontent>
        </c02>
      </c01>
    </dsc>
  </archdesc>
</ead>
```

An EAD portal will use XSLT to transform the above XML record into a human-readable webpage. The designers of the portal will determine important information to be displayed to the users, such as repository information, collection summary, scope and content notes, arrangement notes, access terms, and the list of boxes and folders.

Use of EAD will ensure that archival finding aids created at your institution are interoperable with those created in other institutions. Additionally, many libraries map EAD records to MARC records so that these collections can be found in the library catalog.

Exercise

Create an EAD record for a single collection that contains all photographs from the previous chapter in one folder. The title of the collection is "Photographs from the New Mexico State University Library, MSS 001." The repository is "New Mexico State University Library."

Answer key

```
<ead>
  <eadheader audience="internal" langencoding="iso639-2b">
    <eadid countrycode="us">New Mexico State University
Library</eadid>
    <filedesc>
      <titlestmt>
        <titleproper>Inventory of Photographs from the New
Mexico State University Library</titleproper>
        <author>Processed by A. Jackson, R. Lubas, and I.
Schneider</author>
```

```
      </titlestmt>
      <publicationstmt>
        <publisher>New Mexico State University Library,
Archives and Special Collections</publisher>
        <address><addressline>Archives and Special
Collections</addressline><addressline>4th Floor Branson
Library</addressline><addressline>New Mexico State
University</addressline><addressline>Las Cruces, New
Mexico</addressline></address>
        <date>2012</date>
      </publicationstmt>
    </filedesc>
    <profiledesc>
      <langusage>Finding aid is in <language>English
</language></langusage>
    </profiledesc>
    <revisiondesc>
    </revisiondesc>
  </eadheader>
  <frontmatter>
    <titlepage>
      <titleproper>Inventory of Photographs from the New
Mexico State University Library</titleproper>
      <num>Collection number: MSS 01</num>
      <publisher>New Mexico State University Library,
Archives and Special Collections</publisher>
      <date>Publication date: October 2012</date>
      <list>
        <head>Contact Information</head>
        <item>New Mexico State University Library</item>
        <item>Archives and Special Collections</item>
        <item>New Mexico State University</item>
        <item>Las Cruces, NM</item>
      </list>
      <list>
        <defitem>
          <label>Date processed:</label>
          <item>October 2012</item>
        </defitem>
      </list>
    </titlepage>
```

```
  </frontmatter>
  <archdesc level="collection">
    <did>
      <head>Collection Summary</head>
      <unittitle label="Title">Photographs from the
New Mexico State University Library, <unitdate
type="inclusive"
        >1913-1948</unitdate></unittitle>
      <unitid label="Collection Number">MSS 01</unitid>
      <origination label="Creator">
        <corpname>New Mexico State University Library
</corpname>
      </origination>
      <physdesc label="Size">
        <extent>1 folder (3 photographs)</extent>
      </physdesc>
      <repository label="Repository">
        <corpname>New Mexico State University. Archives and
Special Collections.</corpname>
      </repository>
      <physloc label="Shelf Location">For current
information on the location of these materials, please
inquire at the access desk.</physloc>
      <langmaterial label="Language">
        <language langcode="eng">English.</language>
      </langmaterial>
    </did>
    <scopecontent>
      <head>Scope and Content</head>
      <p>These three photographs are dated from
1913-1948, and are included in The Metadata
Manual: A Practical Workbook for exercises and
examples.</p>
    </scopecontent>
    <bioghist>
      <head>Institutional History</head>
      <p>These photographs, from the New Mexico State
University Library, are included in The Metadata Manual:
A Practical Workbook for exercise examples.</p>
    </bioghist>
    <descgrp type="admininfo">
```

```
      <head>Administrative Information</head>
      <accessrestrict>
        <head>Access Restrictions</head>
        <p>None</p>
      </accessrestrict>
      <userestrict>
        <head>Copy Restrictions</head>
        <p>User responsible for all copyright compliance.
</p>
      </userestrict>
      <prefercite>
        <head>Preferred Citation</head>
        <p>New Mexico State University Library, Archives
and Special Collections, MSS 01</p>
      </prefercite>
    </descgrp>
    <controlaccess>
      <head>Access Terms</head>
      <subject source="lcsh">Motorcycle Machine Gun Corp
</subject>
      <subject source="lcsh"> Machine guns</subject>
      <subject source="lcsh">Motorcycle sidecars</subject>
      <subject source="lcsh"> Hot peppers</subject>
      <subject source="lcsh">Hot pepper industry</subject>
      <geogname>Camel Rock (N.M.)</geogname>
    </controlaccess>
    <dsc type="in-depth">
      <head>Contents List</head>
      <c01 level="item">
        <did>
          <container type="folder">1</container>
          <unittitle>3 photographs from various locations
in New Mexico.</unittitle>
        </did>
      </c01>
    </dsc>
  </archdesc>
</ead>
```

An EAD portal might display the above XML record as seen below after using XSLT to transform the XML into HTML.

Repository: New Mexico State University Library, Archives and Special Collections, Las Cruces, NM

Collection Summary

Title: Photographs from the New Mexico State University Library
Dates: 1913–1948
Creator: Various
Collection Number: Ms 0001
Size: 1 folder (3 photographs)
Repository: New Mexico State University Library
Language: English

Institutional History: These photographs, from the New Mexico State University Library, are included in *The Metadata Manual: A Practical Workbook* for exercise examples.

Scope and Content: These three photographs are dated from 1913-1948, and are included in *The Metadata Manual: A Practical Workbook* for exercises and examples.

Restrictions

Access Restrictions: None
Copy Restrictions: User responsible for all copyright compliance

Administrative Information

Preferred Citation: New Mexico State University Library, Archives and Special Collections, Ms 0001

Access Terms: Camel Rock (N.M.); Motorcycle Machine Gun Corp; Machine guns; Motorcycle sidecars; Hot peppers; Hot pepper industry

Contents List

Description: 3 photographs from various locations in New Mexico

Container: Folder 1

5

Using Categories for the Description of Works of Art (CDWA) and CDWA Lite

With information from the Getty Institute

Abstract: This chapter provides guidelines, advice, and exercises in the usage of Categories for the Description of Works of Art (CDWA) with a focus on the CDWA Lite element set. CDWA is an option for describing images and allows rich description in the metadata record. CDWA was created to provide guidelines for describing works of art, architecture, groups of objects, and visual and textual surrogates. This standard addresses many information needs for the cultural heritage community. A discussion of the content standard Cataloging Cultural Objects (CCO), which interoperates with CDWA, is included. This chapter includes a guide to the element set with description and an exercise.

Key words: CDWA, CDWA Lite, Cataloging Cultural Objects, CCO, digital images, data exchange, cultural works.

Introduction

The Categories for the Description of Works of Art (CDWA) schema is another option for describing images and other works of art. It contains elements useful to describing material objects that may or may not have text included. For example, CDWA distinguishes between "Title" and "Inscription" – a work of art may have an inscription that is not its title. In the image below (Figure 5.1), the title may be composed of part of the

Figure 5.1 **Santa Fe, from Old Fort Marcy**

New Mexico State University Library, Archives and Special Collections

inscription, but there is a great deal of information that will not be included in the title.

CDWA was devised to enable widespread sharing and ingestion in union catalogs, while eliminating much of the overhead associated with shared catalogs (Coburn et al., 2010, p. 18). It has 31 categories and 380 subcategories (Zeng and Qin, 2008, p. 33). CDWA was designed to work with Cataloging Cultural Objects (CCO), and thus is also compatible with popular thesauri such as LCSH and AAT (Art & Architecture Thesaurus) (Boughida, 2005, p. 50).

CDWA was produced by the Art Information Task Force (AITF), which was formed to develop guidelines for describing works of art, architecture, groups of objects, and visual and textual surrogates. Formed in the early 1990s, the Task Force was made up of representatives from the communities that provide and use art information: art historians, museum curators and registrars, visual resource professionals, art librarians, information managers, and technical specialists. The work of the AITF was funded by the J. Paul Getty Trust and the National Endowment for the Humanities (Zeng and Qin, 2008, p. 32).

CDWA contains concepts for creating the framework for your metadata, concepts which are important in the art world: item, group, volume, collection, series, set, and component. Many of them are familiar from other metadata content schemes, such as item and series, but they are tailored to the information needs of the cultural object world.

- Item – the object or work
- Group – an aggregate of items that share a common provenance
- Volume =N materials that are bound together
- Collection =N multiple items arranged together. May not share provenance or binding, but are related in some intellectual way
- Series =N works created in temporal succession
- Set – items intended to be used or viewed as a whole (e.g. a set of globes of the solar system)
- Component – a part of a whole that does not stand alone.

(Zeng and Qin, 2008, p. 34)

CDWA has been mapped to MARC, DC, EAD, and other metadata schemas. If this language meets your collections' needs it can interoperate with many other systems and expose your content to a very wide audience – especially with the creation of CDWA Lite.

CDWA Lite is an XML schema for encoding core records for works of art and material culture. It is a technical interchange standard designed with the needs of art and material culture communities in mind (Baca, 2007, p. 69). CDWA Lite recommends using guidelines from CCO to assist with selecting, ordering, and formatting data used to populate the elements (Coburn et al., 2010, p. 18). If CCO is the content standard, and CDWA is the structural standard, CDWA Lite is the technical structure (Boughida, 2005, p. 50). CDWA Lite fills an important need to deliver the data. It is also a compromise between the richness of CDWA and the sparseness of Dublin Core (Boughida, 2005, p. 52).

CDWA Lite has 22 elements, 19 of which are for descriptive metadata and three of which are for administrative metadata (Coburn et al., 2010, p. 19). Only nine of the elements are required. This standard divides display and indexing elements. CDWA Lite is harvestable via the OAI-PMH standard; thus data in CDWA can be repurposed and easily transported. It is listed as an Open Archives Initiative (OAI) Best Practice. CDWA Lite can be used to share metadata among union catalogs and link back to fuller records with richer description at home institutions (Baca, 2007, p. 70).

CDWA Lite is versatile and can be extended. For example, "Museumdat" is an expansion created by the German Museums Association to provide for the information needs of natural history collections (Coburn et al., 2010, p. 20). The rich standard of CCO coupled with the streamlined CDWA Lite can be a powerful pair to distribute quality metadata describing your art content (Boughida, 2005, p. 53).

CCO (Cataloging Cultural Objects)

The creation of Cataloging Cultural Objects marked the first attempt that had been made to codify content standards for cataloging cultural heritage items (Jackson, 2008, p. 109). The primary focus of CCO is art and architecture, including but not limited to paintings, sculpture, prints, manuscripts, photographs, built works, installations, and other visual media; however, CCO may also cover other types of cultural works, including archaeological sites, artifacts, and functional objects from the realm of material culture. Like AACR2 and DACS, CCO guides cultural heritage professionals in the selection of terms and the order, syntax, and form that descriptive data should take within a data structure (Baca et al., 2006, p. 1). Providing guidance and standardization for the data within a data structure is as important for quality and interoperability as is the standardization of the data structure itself.

CCO has a distinctive concept of what constitutes a work. In CCO, a work is "a distinct intellectual or artistic creation limited primarily to objects and structures made by humans, including built works, visual art works, and cultural artifacts" (Baca et al., 2006, p. 4).

CCO was designed to work with the CDWA and the VRA Core Categories, but can also be used with other structural metadata (Harpring, 2007, p. 34). Historically, CCO evolved from CDWA. This is a marked difference from other content standards such as AACR2, which preceded the creation of corresponding container metadata. CCO was created in the context of container standards being the norm. This standard focuses on descriptive metadata, leaving the administrative and technical elements to CDWA or other structures (Harpring, 2007, p. 34).

CCO is divided into three parts – general guidelines, cataloging rules for work and image elements, and authority work. There are four authority categories in CCO: personal and corporate names, geographic place names, concepts, and subjects. The concept of authorities for names aids in the interoperability of metadata. Agreement on a certain designation for a person, group, place, concept, or subject helps the metadata make sense in context. CCO has core elements that are required or highly recommended, and allows for variation by institution. CCO, like CDWA and VRA, is designed to account for relationships between works.

CCO can be described more as a set of guidelines than a set of rules (Beacom, 2007, p. 82). This traces from its origins, as CCO sought to bring together metadata communities that did not have as long a shared history of a common set of rules as libraries did for textual resources. Its comprehensiveness and flexibility may be a key to widespread adoption as a standard. CCO works well with CDWA Lite and VRA Core 4.0 – in fact, CDWA Lite was designed to be CCO's technical counterpart (Boughida, 2005, p. 53). Becoming familiar with CCO will increase your ability to interact with cultural heritage metadata from other institutions.

Elements

The element definitions contained in this section come from *CDWA Lite: Specification 1.1*, which is maintained by the Getty Research Institute. The specification contains definitions for the 19 descriptive elements and three administrative elements. In addition to the top level elements, there are 28 sub-elements, many of which have sub-elements themselves.

The following list outlines the 19 descriptive elements, 3 administrative elements, and 28 sub-elements. The required elements are in italics. Information on the sub-elements of the sub-elements can be found in the element definitions.

Descriptive metadata

1. **Element:** Object/Work Type Wrapper
   1.1. Sub-element: Object/Work Type
2. **Element:** Title Wrapper
   2.1. Sub-element: Title Set
3. **Element:** Display Creator
4. **Element:** Indexing Creator Wrapper
   4.1. Sub-element: Indexing Creator Set
   4.2. Sub-element: Nationality Creator
   4.3. Sub-element: Vital Dates Creator

4.4. Sub-element: Gender Creator

4.5. Sub-element: Role Creator

4.6. Sub-element: Attribution Qualifier Creator

4.7. Sub-element: Extent Creator

5. **Element:** Display Measurements
6. **Element:** Indexing Measurement Wrapper

   6.1. Sub-element: Indexing Measurement Set

7. **Element:** Display Materials/Techniques
8. **Element:** Indexing Materials/Technique Wrapper

   8.1. Sub-element: Indexing Materials/Techniques Set

9. **Element:** Display State/Edition Wrapper

   9.1. Sub-element: Display State

   9.2. Sub-element: Display Edition

   9.3. Sub-element: Source Display State/Edition

10. **Element:** Style Wrapper

    10.1. Sub-element: Style

11. **Element:** Culture Wrapper

    11.1. Sub-element: Culture

12. **Element:** Display Creation Date
13. **Element:** Indexing Dates Wrapper

    13.1. Sub-element: Indexing Dates Set

14. **Element:** Location/Repository Wrapper

    14.1. Sub-element: Location/Repository Set

15. **Element:** Subject Indexing Wrapper

    15.1. Sub-element: Indexing Subject Set

16. **Element:** Classification Wrapper

    16.1. Sub-element: Classification

17. **Element:** Description/Descriptive Note Wrapper

    17.1. Sub-element: Description/Descriptive Note Set

18. **Element:** Inscriptions Wrapper

    18.1. Sub-element: Inscriptions

19. **Element:** Related Works Wrapper

    19.1. Sub-element: Related Work Set

Administrative metadata

20. **Element:** Rights for Work
21. **Element:** Record Wrapper
    - 21.1. Sub-element: Record ID
    - 21.2. Sub-element: Record Type
    - 21.3. Sub-element: Record Source
    - 21.4. Sub-element: Record Metadata Information Wrapper
22. **Element:** Resource Wrapper
    - 22.1. Sub-element: Resource Set

Element definitions

Descriptive elements

1. **Element:** Object/Work Type Wrapper
   Element tag: <cdwalite:objectWorkTypeWrap>
   Description: A wrapper for Object/Work Type.
   Non-repeatable
   Required

   1.1. **Sub-element: Object/Work Type**
   Element tag: <cdwalite:objectWorkType>
   Description: A term or terms identifying the specific kind of object or work being described. For a collection, include repeatable instances for terms identifying all of or the most important items in the collection.
   Attributes: termsource, termsourceID
   Repeatable
   Required
   Data values: Controlled. Recommended AAT.

2. **Element: Title Wrapper**
   Element tag: <cdwalite:titleWrap>
   Description: Wrapper for Title information.
   Non-repeatable
   Required

   2.1 **Sub-element: Title Set**
   Element tag: <cdwalite:titleSet>

Description: Wrapper for one title and its related information. If there is more than one title, repeat the Title Set element.
Repeatable
Required

2.1.1 **Sub-element: Title**

Element tag:<cdwalite:title>
Description: Titles, identifying phrases, or names given to a work of art, architecture, or material culture. For complex works, series, or collections, the title may refer to a discrete unit within the larger entity (a print from a series, a photograph in a collection, a panel from a fresco cycle, a building within a temple complex) or it may identify only the larger entity (series, collection, cycle) itself.
Attributes: type, pref, lang, langtermsource
Non-repeatable
Required
Data values: Formulated according to data content rules for titles in CCO and CDWA.
Recommended values for preference: preferred, alternate.
Recommended values for type: inscribed, former, translated, repository, traditional, creator, local, and others as recommended in CCO and CDWA.
Recommended values for lang: Language formulated according to rules in the CCO and CDWA (i.e. ISO 639-2b, RFC 3066 and other encoding schemes may be used, or another authoritative source may be used, such as *Ethnologue: Languages of the World.* 14th edition. Barbara F. Grimes, ed. Dallas, Texas: SIL International, 2000). If ISO or other codes are used, they must be translated into common English for end-users.

2.1.2 **Sub-element: Source of Title**

Element tag: <cdwalite:sourceTitle>
Description: The source for the title, generally a published source.
Repeatable
Not required
Data values: Formulated according to rules in the CCO and CDWA.

3. **Element: Display Creator**
   Element tag: <cdwalite:displayCreator>
   Description: The name, brief biographical information, and roles (if necessary) of the named creator or creators in the design and production of the work, presented in a syntax suitable for display to the end-user and including any necessary indications of uncertainty, ambiguity, and nuance. If there is no known creator, make a reference to the presumed culture or nationality of the unknown creator.
   Non-repeatable
   Required
   Data values: Formulated according to data content rules for creator display in CCO and CDWA; may be concatenated from the Indexing Creator elements, if necessary. The name should be in natural order, if possible, although inverted order is acceptable. Include nationality and life dates. For unknown creators, use one of the conventions illustrated in the following examples: "unknown," "unknown Chinese," "Chinese," or "unknown 15th-century Chinese."

4. **Element: Indexing Creator Wrapper**
   Element tag: <cdwalite:indexingCreatorWrap>
   Description: Wrapper for one or more sets of Indexing Creator elements.
   Non-repeatable
   Required

   4.1 Sub-element: Indexing Creator Set
   Element tag: <cdwalite:indexingCreatorSet>
   Description: Wrapper for creator indexing elements. If there are multiple creators, repeat Indexing Creator Set.
   Repeatable
   Required

   4.1.1 Sub-element: Name Creator Set
   Element tag: <cdwalite:nameCreatorSet>
   Description: Wrapper for name elements. If there are multiple names for a creator, repeat the Name Creator Set.
   Repeatable
   Required

   4.1.1.1 Sub-element: Name of Creator
   Element tag: <cdwalite:nameCreator>

Attributes: type, termsource termsourceID

Description: The names, appellations, or other identifiers assigned to an individual, group of people, firm or other corporate body, or other entity that has contributed to the design, creation, production, manufacture, or alteration of the work.

Non-repeatable

Required

Comment: Use of a Personal and Corporate Name Authority, from which the names, nationality, and dates may be derived, is recommended. See CCO A1: Personal and Corporate Name Authority.

Data values: Controlled. For name, recommended: ULAN and AAAF (LC authority files).

Data values for type attribute: personalName, corporateName.

4.1.1.2 Sub-element: Source of Name Creator

Element tag: <cdwalite:sourceNameCreator>

Description: The source for the name, generally a published source.

Repeatable

Not required

Data values: Formulated according to rules in the CCO and CDWA.

4.2 Sub-element: Nationality Creator

Element tag: <cdwalite:nationalityCreator>

Description: National or cultural affiliation of the person or corporate body.

Repeatable

Not required

Note: While not required, it is highly recommended to include the nationality.

Data values: Controlled. Recommended: TGN, AAT.

4.3 Sub-element: Vital Dates Creator

Element tag: <cdwalite:vitalDatesCreator>

Attributes: birthdate, deathdate, termsource

Description: A description of the lifespan of the person or the existence of the corporate body, using “ca.” and any other expressions of uncertainty or nuance. For Birth and Death date

attributes, record years of birth and death, estimated where necessary. For a corporate body, use birthdate and deathdate to record the dates of founding and dissolution.
Repeatable
Not required
Note: While not required, it is highly recommended to include birth and death dates.
Data values: Indexing dates should be formulated according to the rules in CCO and CDWA. Format will vary depending upon implementation. (Do not repeat attributes birthdate or deathdate within one set of Vital Dates.)

4.4 **Sub-element: Gender Creator**
Element tag: <cdwalite:genderCreator>
Description: The sex of the individual. Not applicable for corporate bodies.
Non-repeatable
Not required
Data values: male, female, unknown, not applicable, as recommended in CCO and CDWA.

4.5 **Sub-element: Role Creator**
Element tag: <cdwalite:roleCreator>
Description: The role played by the creator or other agent in the creation or production of the work.
Attributes: termsource, termsourceID
Repeatable
Required
Data values for role: Controlled. Recommended: AAT. Default = artist.

4.6 **Sub-element: Attribution Qualifier Creator**
Element tag: <cdwalite:attributionQualifierCreator>
Description: A qualifier used when the attribution is uncertain, is in dispute, when there is more than one creator, when there is a former attribution, or when the attribution otherwise requires explanation.
Repeatable
Not required
Data values: attributed to, studio of, workshop of, atelier of, office of, assistant of, associate of, pupil of, follower of, school of, circle of, style of, after, copyist of, manner of, used according to the recommendations in CCO and CDWA.

4.7 **Sub-element: Extent Creator**
Element tag: <cdwalite:extentCreator>
Description: When there are multiple creators, a term indicating the part of the work created by this creator.
Repeatable
Not required
Data values: design, execution, with additions by, figures, renovation by, predella, embroidery, cast by, printed by, and others as recommended in CCO and CDWA.

5. **Element: Display Measurements**
Element tag: <cdwalite:displayMeasurements>
Description: Information about the dimensions, size, or scale of the work, presented in a syntax suitable for display to the end-user and including any necessary indications of uncertainty, ambiguity, and nuance. It may include the scale of the work. It may also include the number of the parts of a complex work, series, or collection.
Non-repeatable
Not required
Note: While not required, it is highly recommended to include display measurements.
Data values: Formulated according to data content rules for measurements in CCO and CDWA; generally presented height by width by depth, unless otherwise indicated. Metric units preferred, with values in inches as well, if possible. May be concatenated from controlled fields.

6. **Element: Indexing Measurements Wrapper**
Element tag: <cdwalite:indexingMeasurementsWrap>
Description: A wrapper for the Indexing Measurements.
Non-repeatable
Not required

6.1 **Sub-element: Indexing Measurements Set**
Element tag: <cdwalite:indexingMeasurementsSet>
Description: The dimensions, size, shape, scale, format, or storage configuration of the work, including volume, weight, area, or running time. Measurements are formatted to allow retrieval; preferably in metric units where applicable; if multiple parts of the work are measured, repeat the Indexing Measurements Set element.
Repeatable
Not required

6.1.1 Sub-element: Measurement Set

Element tag: <cdwalite:measurementsSet>

Attributes: value, unit, type

Description: The dimensions or other measurements for one aspect of a work (e.g. width); may be combined with extent, qualifier, and other sub-elements as necessary.

Repeatable

Not required

Data values for value: whole numbers or decimal fractions.

Data values for unit: cm, mm, m, g, kg, kb, Mb, Gb, and others as recommended in CCO and CDWA.

Data values for type: height, width, depth, length, diameter, circumference, stories, count, area, volume, running time, size (e.g. US Women's size 8), base, target, and others as recommended in CCO and CDWA.

6.1.2 Sub-element: Extent Measurements

Element tag: <cdwalite:extentMeasurements>

Description: An explanation of the part of the work being measured; included when necessary for clarity.

Repeatable

Not required

Data values: overall, components, sheet, plate mark, chain lines, pattern repeat, lid, base, laid lines, folios, leaves, columns per page, lines per page, tessera, footprint, panel, interior, mat, window of mat, secondary support, frame, mount, and others as recommended in CCO and CDWA.

6.1.3 Sub-element: Qualifier Measurements

Element tag: <cdwalite:qualifierMeasurements>

Description: A word or phrase that elaborates on the nature of the measurements of the work when necessary, as when the measurements are approximate.

Repeatable

Not required

Data values: approximate, sight, maximum, largest, smallest, average, variable, assembled, before restoration, at corners, rounded, framed with base, and others as recommended in CCO and CDWA.

6.1.4 Sub-element: Format Measurements

Element tag: <cdwalite:formatMeasurements>

Description: The configuration of a work, including technical formats, used as necessary.
Repeatable
Not required
Data values: cabinet photograph, vignette, VHS, IMAX, DOS, and others as recommended in CCO and CDWA.

6.1.5 **Sub-element: Shape Measurements**
Element tag: <cdwalite:shapeMeasurements>
Description: The shape of a work, used for unusual shapes (e.g. an oval painting).
Repeatable
Not required
Data values: oval, round, square, rectangular, irregular, and others as recommended in CCO and CDWA.

6.1.6 **Sub-element: Scale Measurements**
Element tag: <cdwalite:scaleMeasurements>
Description: An expression of the ratio between the size of the representation of something and that thing (e.g. the size of the drawn structure and the actual built work). Used for studies, record drawings, models, and other representations drawn or constructed to scale.
Repeatable
Not required
Data values for scale: numeric (e.g. 1 inch = 1 foot), full-size, life-size, half-size, monumental, and others as recommended in CCO and CDWA. Combine this tag with Measurement Sets for numeric scales. For measurementsSet type for Scale, use "base" for the left side of the equation, and "target" for the right side of the equation.

7. **Element: Display Materials/Techniques**
Element tag: <cdwalite:displayMaterialsTech>
Description: An indication of the substances or materials used in the creation of a work, as well as any implements, production or manufacturing techniques, processes, or methods incorporated in its fabrication, presented in a syntax suitable for display to the end-user and including any necessary indications of uncertainty, ambiguity, and nuance. For works on paper, descriptions of watermarks may also be included. (For marks applied to the work or support by the artist or subsequently by another person, see Inscriptions.)

Non-repeatable
Required
Data values: Formulated according to data content rules for materials in CCO and CDWA. May be concatenated from controlled fields, if necessary.

8. **Element: Indexing Materials/Technique Wrapper**
   Element tag: <cdwalite:indexingMaterialsTechWrap>
   Description: A wrapper for Indexing Materials/Techniques.
   Non-repeatable
   Not required

   8.1 **Sub-element: Indexing Materials/Techniques Set**
   Element tag: <cdwalite:indexingMaterialsTechSet>
   Description: Materials and techniques indexed with controlled terms for retrieval; if multiple parts of the work require separate materials and techniques, or if you are recording media and support separately, repeat this element with the type attribute and/or the extent sub-element.
   Attribute: type
   Repeatable
   Not required
   Data values for type: medium, support, technique, material, implement, mark (e.g. watermark or other mark inherent in the material).

   8.1.1 **Sub-element: Term Materials Techniques**
   Element tag: <cdwalite:termMaterialsTech>
   Description: A term to index materials and/or technique; may be combined with extent as necessary.
   Attributes: termsource, termsourceID
   Repeatable
   Not required
   Data values: Controlled. Recommended: AAT.

   8.1.2 **Sub-element: Extent Materials Techniques**
   Element tag: <cdwalite:extentMaterialsTech>
   Description: An explanation of the part of the work to which the materials or technique are applicable; included when necessary for clarity.
   Repeatable
   Not required

8.1.3 Sub-element: Source Materials Techniques
Element tag: <cdwalite:sourceMaterialsTech>
Description: The source of the information about materials and technique, often used when citing a published source of watermarks.
Repeatable
Not required
Data values: Formulated according to rules in the CCO and CDWA.

9. Element: Display State/Edition Wrapper
Element tag: <displayStateEditionWrap>
Non-repeatable
Not required

9.1 Sub-element: Display State
Element tag: <cdwalite:displayState>
Description: A description of the state of the work; used primarily for prints and other multiples.
Non-repeatable
Not required
Data values: Formulated according to rules in the CCO and CDWA. For State, include state identification and known states, as appropriate.

9.2 Sub-element: Display Edition
Element tag: <cdwalite:displayEdition>
Description: A description of the edition of the work; used primarily for prints and other multiples.
Non-repeatable
Not required
Data values: Formulated according to rules in the CCO and CDWA. For Edition, include impression number, edition size, and edition number, or edition name, as appropriate.

9.3 Sub-element: Source Display State/Edition
Element tag: <cdwalite:sourceStateEdition>
Description: The published source of the state or edition information.
Repeatable
Not required
Data values: Formulated according to rules in the CCO and CDWA.

10. **Element: Style Wrapper**
    Element tag: <cdwalite:styleWrap>
    Description: A wrapper for style elements.
    Non-repeatable
    Not required

    10.1 **Sub-element: Style**
        Element tag: <cdwalite:style>
        Description: Term that identifies the named, defined style, historical or artistic period, movement, group, or school whose characteristics are represented in the work being catalogued.
        Attributes: termsource, termsourceID
        Repeatable
        Not required
        Data values: Controlled. Recommended: AAT.

11. **Element: Culture Wrapper**
    Element tag: <cdwalite:cultureWrap>
    Description: A wrapper for Culture elements.
    Non-repeatable
    Not required

    11.1 **Sub-element: Culture**
        Element tag: <cdwalite:culture>
        Description: Name of the culture, people, or nationality from which the work originated.
        Attributes: termsource, termsourceID
        Repeatable
        Not required
        Data values: Controlled. Recommended: AAT, TGN.

12. **Element: Display Creation Date**
    Element tag: <cdwalite:displayCreationDate>
    Description: A concise description of the date or range of dates associated with the creation, design, production, presentation, performance, construction, or alteration of the work or its components, presented in a syntax suitable for display to the end-user and including any necessary indications of uncertainty, ambiguity, and nuance.
    Non-repeatable
    Required
    Data values: Formulated according to data content rules for display dates in CCO and CDWA. May be concatenated from controlled fields, if necessary.

13. **Element: Indexing Dates Wrapper**
Element tag: <indexingDatesWrap>
Description: A wrapper for Indexing Dates.
Non-repeatable
Required

13.1 **Sub-element: Indexing Dates Set**
Element tag: <cdwalite:indexingDatesSet>
Description: A wrapper for one set of years in the proleptic Gregorian calendar delimiting the span of time during which the creation and production of the work took place, as indicated in the Display Creation Date. If the creation took place in a single year, repeat the same year in earliest and latest dates. For ca. and other uncertain or approximate dates, estimate the greatest possible span for indexing, as recommended in CCO and CDWA. If different parts of the work were done at different times, or if different activities in the production of the work were done at different times, repeat Indexing Dates Set.
Repeatable
Required

13.1.1 **Sub-element: Date Qualifier**
Element tag: <cdwalite:dateQualifier>
Description: A clarification of the meaning of the date, used when necessary.
Non-repeatable
Not required
Data values: design, execution, alteration, performance, restoration, destruction, discovery, and others as described in CCO and CDWA.

13.1.2 **Sub-element: Earliest Date**
Element tag: <cdwalite:earliestDate>
Description: A year that broadly delimits the beginning of an implied date span.
Attribute: termsource
Non-repeatable
Required
Data values: Indexing dates should be formulated according to the rules in CCO and CDWA. Format will vary depending upon implementation.

13.1.3 **Sub-element: Latest Date**
Element tag: <cdwalite:latestDate>
Description: A year that broadly delimits the end of an implied date span.
Attribute: termsource
Non-repeatable
Required
Data values: Indexing dates should be formulated according to the rules in CCO and CDWA. Format will vary depending upon implementation.

14. **Element: Location/Repository Wrapper**
Element tag: <cdwalite:locationWrap>
Description: A wrapper for Location/Repository information.
Non-repeatable
Required

14.1 **Sub-element: Location/Repository Set**
Element tag: <cdwalite:locationSet>
Description: A wrapper for the location name and ID. If there are multiple locations, repeat this element.
Repeatable
Required

14.1.1 **Sub-element: Location/Repository Name**
Element tag: <cdwalite:locationName>
Description: The name and geographic location of the repository that is currently responsible for the work, or, for monumental works and architecture, the geographic location of the work. If the work is lost, destroyed, has location unknown, or the work is in an anonymous private collection, indicate this. Also may include creation location, discovery location, and other former locations.
Attributes: type, termsource, termsourceID, locID, locIDtype
Non-repeatable
Required
Comment: The locID attribute is the code that uniquely identifies the repository.
Data values: Controlled. BHA (Bibliography of the History of Art) index, Anglo-American Authority Files

(AAAF) (LC authorities and subject headings), Grove's Dictionary of Art Location Appendix, International Directory of the Arts, Official Museum Directory, and TGN. Use of separate authorities for corporate bodies and geographic locations is recommended. See the discussion in CCO and CDWA. Other terminology as necessary: lost, destroyed, location unknown, private collection.

Recommended values for type: currentLocation, currentRepository, formerRepository, currentArchitectural Context, formerArchitecturalContext, currentGeographic, formerGeographic, discoveryLocation, creationLocation.

14.1.2 **Sub-element: Repository Work Identification Number**

Element tag: <cdwalite:workID>

Description: Any unique numeric or alphanumeric identifier(s) assigned to a work by a repository.

Attribute: type

Repeatable

Not required

Note: While not required, it is highly recommended to include work identification number if known.

Recommended values for type attribute: accession, shelfNumber, objectId, and others as recommended in CCO and CDWA.

15. **Element: Subject Indexing Wrapper**

Element tag: <cdwalite:indexingSubjectWrap>

Description: A wrapper for Subject Indexing information about the work, group, collection, or series that is being catalogued.

Non-repeatable

Not required

15.1 **Sub-element: Indexing Subject Set**

Element tag: <cdwalite:indexingSubjectSet>

Description: A wrapper for one set of Subject Indexing information. If a work has multiple parts or otherwise has separate, multiple subjects, repeat this element with Extent Subject. This element may also be repeated to distinguish between subjects that reflect what a work is "of" (description and identification) from what it is "about" (interpretation).

Attributes: type

Repeatable
Not required
Data Values: For type, values may include description, identification, interpretation; for use if necessary to distinguish between what a work is "of" and what it is "about."

15.1.1 **Sub-element: Extent Subject**
Element tag: <cdwalite:extentSubject>
Description: When there are multiple subjects, a term indicating the part of the work to which these subject terms apply.
Non-repeatable
Not required
Data Values: recto, verso, side A, side B, main panel, predella, and others as described in CCO and CDWA.

15.1.2 **Sub-element: Indexing Subject Term**
Element tag: <cdwalite:subjectTerm>
Description: Terms that identify, describe, and/or interpret what is depicted in and by a work. These may include proper names (e.g. people, events, places), iconography, themes from literature, or generic terms describing the material world, or topics (e.g. concepts, themes, or issues).
Attributes: type, termsource, termsourceID
Repeatable
Not required
Note: While not required, it is highly recommended to include subject terms, even for non-objective art, for which the function or purpose of the work may be included as subject.
Data values: Controlled. Recommended AAT, TGN, LC Name and Subject Authorities, TGM (Library of Congress Thesaurus for Graphic Materials), Iconclass, Sears Subject Headings. Derive terminology from authoritative sources, where possible. See the list of sources in CCO and CDWA. Use of a Subject Authority and other authorities from which these data values may be derived is recommended.
Recommended values type attribute: conceptTerm, iconography, eventName, personalName, corporate BodyName, geographicName.

16. **Element: Classification Wrapper**
Element tag: <cdwalite:classificationWrap>
Description: A wrapper for classification information.
Non-repeatable
Not required

16.1 **Sub-element: Classification**
Element tag: <cdwalite:classification>
Description: Term used to categorize a work by grouping it together with other works on the basis of similar characteristics, including materials, form, shape, function, region of origin, cultural context, or historical or stylistic period. If the work is assigned to multiple classifications, repeat this element.
Attributes: termsource, termsourceID
Repeatable
Not required
Data values: Controlled. Recommended: AAT.

17. **Element: Description/Descriptive Note Wrapper**
Element tag: <cdwalite:descriptiveNoteWrap>
Description: A wrapper for Description/Descriptive Note information.
Non-repeatable
Not required

17.1 **Sub-element: Description/Descriptive Note Set**
Element tag: <cdwalite:descriptiveNoteSet>
Description: A wrapper for a descriptive note and its sources. If there is more than one descriptive note, repeat this sub-element.
Repeatable
Not required

17.1.1 **Sub-element: Description/Descriptive Note**
Element tag: <cdwalite:descriptiveNote>
Description: A relatively brief essay-like text that describes the content and context of the work, including comments and an interpretation that may supplement, qualify, or explain the physical characteristics, subject, circumstances of creation or discovery, or other information about the work.
Non-repeatable
Not required
Data values: Formulated according to data content rules for the Description element in CCO and CDWA.

17.1.2 **Sub-element: Source Description/Descriptive Note**
Element tag: <cdwalite:sourceDescriptiveNote>
Description: The source for the descriptive note, generally a published source.
Repeatable
Not required
Data values: Formulated according to rules in the CCO and CDWA.

18. **Element: Inscriptions Wrapper**
Element tag: <cdwalite:inscriptionsWrap>
Description: A wrapper for Inscription information.
Non-repeatable
Not required

18.1 **Sub-element: Inscriptions**
Element tag: <cdwalite:inscriptions>
Description: A description or transcription of any distinguishing or identifying physical lettering, annotations, texts, markings, or labels that are affixed, applied, stamped, written, inscribed, or attached to the work, excluding any mark or text inherent in the materials of which the work is made (record watermarks in Display Materials/Techniques).
Repeatable
Not required
Data values: Formulated according to data content rules for Inscriptions in CCO and CDWA.

19. **Element: Related Works Wrapper**
Element tag: <cdwalite:relatedWorksWrap>
Description: A wrapper for Related Works information.
Non-repeatable
Not required

19.1 **Sub-element: Related Work Set**
Element tag: <cdwalite:relatedWorkSet>
Description: A wrapper for one work, group, collection, or series that is directly related to the work at hand, including direct relationships between two works, between a work and its components, and between an item and the larger group, collection, or series of works. Related works may also include works that were created as pendants or otherwise to be displayed together with the work at hand. If there is more

than one Related Work for the work being catalogued, repeat this element.
Repeatable
Not required

19.1.1 **Sub-element: Link Related Work**
Element tag: <cdwalite:linkRelatedWork>
Description: A URI/URL reference that is universal and in the World Wide Web environment.
Attribute: linkscheme
Repeatable
Not required
Data values: From data in the generating system (e.g. marc0359).

19.1.2 **Sub-element: Related Work Relationship Type**
Element tag: <cdwalite:relatedWorkRelType>
Description: A term describing the nature of the relationship between the work at hand and the related entity.
Non-repeatable
Not required
Recommended values: part of, larger context for, model of, model for, study of, study for, rendering of, copy of, etc., as discussed in CCO and CDWA (Part 1). The default is related to.
Note: For implementation of the data: note that relationships are conceptually reciprocal, but the Relationship Type is often different on either side of the relationship (e.g. one work is part of a second work, but, from the point of view of the second record, the first work is the larger context for the second work). Whether or not relationships are physically reciprocal as implemented in systems is a local decision.

19.1.3 **Sub-element: Label for Related Work/Group/Collection/Series**
Element tag: <cdwalite:labelRelatedWork>
Description: An identification of the related work, group, collection, or series that will be meaningful to end-users, including some or all of the following information, as necessary for clarity and if known: title,

creator, object/work type, and creation date. Display it with the Location of Related Work.
Repeatable
Not required
Data values: Ideally generated from fields/elements in the related record.

19.1.4 **Sub-element: Location of Related Work**
Element tag: <cdwalite:locRelatedWork>
Description: The current location of the related work, generally a repository or, for architecture and monumental works, a geographic place. For series and other works published in multiples, location may not be applicable.
Attributes: relWorkID, locID, locIDtype, termSource
Repeatable
Not required
Data values: Ideally generated from fields/elements in the related record.
Comment: The relWorkID attribute is the repository's unique numeric or alphanumeric identifier for the work. The locIDtype is the authoritative source that supplied the locID. The locID attribute is the unique code identifying this repository.

Administrative elements

20. **Element: Rights for Work**
Element tag: <cdwalite:rightsWork>
Description: Information about rights management; may include copyright and other intellectual property statements required for use regarding the work. If the holder of the reproduction rights to the image/resource differs from the rights for the work, use rightsResource described below.
Attribute: type
Repeatable
Not required

21. **Element: Record Wrapper**
Element tag: <cdwalite:recordWrap>
Description: A wrapper for information about the record that contains the cataloging information.

Non-repeatable
Required

21.1 **Sub-element: Record ID**
Element tag: <cdwalite:recordID>
Description: A unique record identification in the contributor's (local) system.
Attribute: type
Repeatable
Required

21.2 **Sub-element: Record Type**
Element tag: <cdwalite:recordType>
Description: Term establishing whether the record represents an individual item or a collection, series, or group of works.
Non-repeatable
Required
Note: It is required to designate the Record type. The default is item.
Data Values: item, collection, series, group, volume, fonds, and other values as necessary, as described in the CCO and the CDWA.

21.3 **Sub-element: Record Source**
Element tag: <cdwalite:recordSource>
Description: The source of information in this record, generally the repository or other institution.
Repeatable
Not required
Data values: Formulated according to rules in the CCO and CDWA.

21.4 **Sub-element: Record Metadata Information Wrapper**
Element tag: <cdwalite:recordInfoWrap>
Description: Wrapper for metadata information about this record.
Attribute: type
Repeatable
Not required

21.4.1 **Sub-element: Record Info ID**
Element tag: <cdwalite:recordInfoID>
Description: Unique ID of the metadata. Record Info ID has the same definition as Record ID but out of the

context of original local system, such as a persistent identifier or an oai identifier (e.g. oai1:getty.edu:paintings/00001234 attribute type= oai).
Attribute: type
Repeatable
Not required

21.4.2 **Sub-element: Record Info Link**
Element tag: <cdwalite:recordinfoLink>
Description: Link of the metadata (not the same as link of the object).
Repeatable
Not required

21.4.3 **Sub-element: Record Relationship ID**
Element tag: <cdwalite:recordRelID>
Description: Unique ID of the metadata of the related object.
Attribute: type
Repeatable
Not required

21.4.4 **Sub-element: Record Metadata Location**
Element tag: <cdwalite:recordMetadataLoc>
Description: Pointer(s) to other metadata (administrative, technical, structural).
Attribute: type
Repeatable
Not required

21.4.5 **Sub-element: Record Metadata Date**
Element tag: <cdwalite:recordMetadataDate>
Description: creation date or date modified.
Attribute: type
Repeatable
Not required
Data values: Format will vary depending upon implementation.

22. **Element: Resource Wrapper**
Element tag: <cdwalite:resourceWrap>
Description: A wrapper for information about the images or other resources that serve as visual surrogates of the work, including digital

images, slides, transparencies, photographs, videos, audio, and moving images, but excluding items that are considered works in their own right. For works such as drawings, prints, paintings, or photographs considered art, and other works that themselves contain representations of other works, use Related Works and/or Subjects.
Non-repeatable
Not required
Note: For discussion regarding the Resource, see Image in CCO and Related Visual Documentation in CDWA.

22.1 **Sub-element: Resource Set**
Element tag: <cdwalite:resourceSet>
Description: A wrapper for sets of resource information. If there are multiple resources associated with the work, repeat the Resource Set sub-element.
Repeatable
Not required

22.1.1 **Sub-element: Link Resource**
Element tag: <cdwalite:linkResource>
Description: A URI/URL reference that is universal and in the World Wide Web environment.
Attributes: type, formatresource
Non-repeatable
Not required

22.1.2 **Sub-element: Resource Identification Number**
Element tag: <cdwalite:resourceID>
Description: The unique numeric or alphanumeric identification of the resource.
Attribute: type
Non-repeatable
Not required

22.1.3 **Resource Relationship Type**
Element tag: <cdwalite:resourceRelType>
Description: The relationship of an image or other resource to the work being described.
Repeatable
Not required
Data values: conservation image, documentary image, contextual image, historical image, reconstruction, installation image, and others as discussed in CDWA.

22.1.4 **Resource Type**

Element tag: <cdwalite:resourceType>

Attributes: termsource, termsourceID

Description: The generic identification of the medium of the image or other resource.

Repeatable

Not required

Data values: Controlled. Recommended AAT. Digital image, photograph, slide, videotape, X-ray photograph, negative, internegative, albumen print, duplicate slide, and others as discussed in CDWA.

22.1.5 **Sub-element: Rights for Resource**

Element tag: <cdwalite:rightsResource>

Description: Information about rights regarding the image or other resource. Use this sub-element if the holder of the reproduction rights for the image/resource differs from the holder of rights for the work. See also Rights Work above. (For example, the work rights are "©national Museum of African Art, Smithsonian Institution (Washington DC)," but the image rights are "Photo © Frank Khoury.")

Repeatable

Not required

22.1.6 **Sub-element: Resource View Description**

Element tag: <cdwalite:resourceViewDescription>

Description: A description of the spatial, chronological, or contextual aspects of the work as captured in the view of this particular image or other resource.

Non-repeatable

Not required

22.1.7 **Sub-element: Resource View Type**

Element tag: <cdwalite:resourceViewType>

Description: The specific vantage point or perspective of the view.

Attributes: termsource, termsourceID

Repeatable

Not required

Data values: Controlled. Recommended AAT.

22.1.8 **Sub-element: Resource View Subject Term**
Element tag: <cdwalite:resourceViewSubjectTerm>
Description: Terms or phrases that characterize the subject matter of the work as it is depicted in a specific image or other resource.
Attributes: type, termsource, termsourceID
Repeatable
Not required
Data values: Controlled. Recommended AAT, TGN, LC Name and Subject Authorities, TGM, Iconclass, Sears Subject Headings. Derive terminology from authoritative sources, where possible. See the list of sources in CCO and CDWA. Data values may be derived from a Subject Authority and other authorities.
Recommended values type attribute: conceptTerm, iconography, eventName, personalName, corporateBodyName, geographicName.

22.1.9 **Sub-element: Resource View Date**
Element tag: <cdwalite:resourceViewDate>
Description: A date or range of dates associated with the creation or production of the image. This is not necessarily the same as the date of production of the resource (e.g. a print of a negative may be made years after the image was first captured on film). For the date of the resource, use Resource Date.
Attributes: earliestdate, latestdate, termsource
Non-repeatable
Not required
Data values: Indexing dates should be formulated according to the rules in CCO and CDWA. Format will vary depending upon implementation.

22.1.10 **Sub-element: Resource Source**
Element tag: <cdwalite:resourceSource>
Description: Identification of the agency, individual, repository, or publication from which the image or other resource was obtained, including a bibliographic citation in the case of copy photography. Include this sub-element when the source of the image/resource differs from the source named in Record Source.

Repeatable
Not required
Data values: Formulated according to rules in CDWA.

22.1.11 **Sub-element: Link Related Resource**
Element tag: <cdwalite:linkRelatedResource>
Description: A reference to an image or other resource that is related to the resource in this Resource Set, generally linking a group or collection of images or other resources to members of the group or collection. For multiple related resources, repeat this element.
Attribute: linkscheme
Repeatable
Not required

22.1.11.1 **Sub-element: Related Resource Relationship Type**
Element tag: <cdwalite:relatedResourceRel Type>
Description: A term describing the nature of the relationship between the resource at hand and the related resource.
Non-repeatable
Not required
Recommended values: part of, larger context for, related to, and other values as needed.

22.1.11.2 **Sub-element: Label for Related Resource**
Element tag: <cdwalite:labelRelatedResou rce>
Description: An identification of the related image or other resource that will be meaningful to end-users.
Repeatable
Not required

22.1.12 **Sub-element: Resource Metadata Location**
Element tag: <cdwalite:resourceMetadataLoc>
Description: Pointer(s) to other metadata (administrative, technical, structural).
Attribute: type
Repeatable
Not required

Example record

Figure 5.2 **Boat landing and Elephant Butte**

New Mexico State University Library, Archives and Special Collections

Available information (from a Dublin Core description of the digital image):
Title: Boat landing and Elephant Butte
Subject: Elephant Butte Reservoir (N.M.)
Description: Caption on image reads, "Boat landing and Elephant Butte, Elephant Butte Dam, New Mexico." Logo stamped next to caption reads, "Frashers Fotos." Image showing the Elephant Butte Reservoir with Elephant Butte rising out of the water. A boat ramp and a number of boats are visible in the reservoir in the bottom left corner of the image.
Publisher: New Mexico State University Library
Date Digital: 2003-11-12
Type: Still Image
Format: image/jpeg
Digitization Specifications: 8 bits, 300 dpi
Identifier: Ms02231516
Source: Gelatin silver postcard

Language: eng
Collection: Thomas K. Todsen Photographs, Collection No. Ms 0223
Rights: Copyright, NMSU Board of Regents. Please send questions to: archives@lib.nmsu.edu

Object/Work Type: digital image
Title: Boat landing and Elephant Butte
Display Creator: unknown American
Name of Creator: unknown
Nationality Creator: American
Role Creator: photographer
Format Measurements: JPEG
Display Materials/Techniques: digital imaging
Indexing Materials/Techniques:
  Term Materials Techniques: digital imaging
Display Creation Date: 2003-11-12
Location/Repository Name:
  Type: currentRepository: New Mexico State University Library
Indexing Subject Term: Elephant Butte Reservoir (N.M.)
Description/Descriptive Note: Image showing the Elephant Butte Reservoir with Elephant Butte rising out of the water. A boat ramp and a number of boats are visible in the reservoir in the bottom left corner of the image.
Inscriptions: Handwritten caption on image reads, "Boat landing and Elephant Butte, Elephant Butte Dam, New Mexico." Logo stamped next to caption reads, "Frashers Fotos."
Related Work Relationship Type: related to
Label for Related Work: Ms02231516
Related Collection Relationship Type: part of
Label for Related Collection: Ms0223, Thomas K. Todsen Photographs
Location of Related Collection: New Mexico State University Library
Rights for Work: Copyright, NMSU Board of Regents

Exercises

The following exercises present a surrogate of an original work (Figure 5.3), held by the New Mexico State University Library, along with the information available to the metadata cataloger.

Exercise 5.1

Figure 5.3 **Scene at Santa Fe Station**

New Mexico State University Library, Archives and Special Collections

Available information:

- Description: Scene at Santa Fe Station
- Date: 20 December 1935 (postmark)
- Notes: Published by Strong's Book Store, Albuquerque, New Mexico; copyrighted by C. T. & Company, Chicago, Illinois; from souvenir folder of Albuquerque, New Mexico
- Collection: Thomas K. Todsen Photographs
- Collection Number: Ms0223
- Physical Description: photomechanical color print

Exercise 5.2

Available information:

- Description: Automobile Road on La Bajada Hill on "Ocean to Ocean Scenic Highway"
- Location: Near Santa Fe, New Mexico
- Date: 1 March 1913 (postmark)
- Notes: Published by Jesse L. Nusbaum, Santa Fe, New Mexico
- Collection: Thomas K. Todsen Photographs

Figure 5.4 **Automobile Road on La Bajada Hill**

New Mexico State University Library, Archives and Special Collections

- Collection Number: Ms0223
- Physical Description: tinted photomechanical post card

Exercise 5.3

Available information (from a Dublin Core description of the digital image):

- Title: Danzante (matachin) group
- Subject: Matachines (Dance)
- Description: Description in older database reads, "Danzante (matachin) group. Man third from right is Cenovio Avalos, second from right is Francisco Dominguez. Las Cruces or Tortugas, New Mexico."
- Publisher: New Mexico State University Library
- Date original: 1907?
- Date Digital: 2009-02-19
- Type: Still Image
- Format: image/jpeg
- Digitization Specifications: Adobe Photoshop CS3 Macintosh; 8 bits; 300 dpi
- Identifier: Ms00040260

Figure 5.5 **Danzante (matachin) group**

New Mexico State University Library, Archives and Special Collections

- Source: Glass negative
- Collection: Amador Family Papers, Collection No. Ms 0004; guide available at *http://rmoa.unm.edu/docviewer.php?docId=nmlcu1ms4.xml*
- Rights: Copyright, NMSU Board of Regents. Please send questions to: archives@lib.nmsu.edu
- Contributing Institution: New Mexico State University Library, Archives and Special Collections Department, Rio Grande Historical Collections

Answer key

The production of metadata can sometimes be very subjective, and the fullness of the metadata produced will depend on the amount of information available to the metadata cataloger. However, the following items provide an example of the metadata that could be produced for the above exercises.

Exercise 5.1
Scene at Santa Fe Station

- Object/Work Type: digital image
- Title: Scene at Santa Fe Station
- Display Creator: unknown American
- Name of Creator: unknown
- Nationality Creator: American
- Role Creator: artist
- Format Measurements: JPEG
- Display Materials/Techniques: digital imaging
- Indexing Materials/Techniques
- Term Materials Techniques: digital imaging
- Display Creation Date: unknown
- Date Qualifier: Date of original
- Earliest Date: unknown
- Latest Date: 1935-12
- Location/Repository Name:

- Type: currentRepository: New Mexico State University Library
- Indexing Subject Term: Train stations; Santa Fe (N.M.)
- Description/Descriptive Note: Image showing a scene from the courtyard of the Santa Fe Station in Santa Fe, New Mexico.
- Inscriptions: Handwritten captions along top read "[Ms223, 466]" and "[RG88-168]." Printed caption on the bottom reads, "Scene at Santa Fe Station." Older database indicates the original item is a photomechanical color print.
- Related Work Relationship Type: related to
- Label for Related Work: Ms02230466
- Related Collection Relationship Type: part of
- Label for Related Collection: Ms0223, Thomas K. Todsen Photographs
- Location of Related Collection: New Mexico State University Library
- Rights for Work: Copyright NMSU Board of Regents

Exercise 5.2
Automobile Road on La Bajada Hill

- Object/Work Type: digital image
- Title: Automobile road on La Bajada Hill
- Display Creator: unknown American
- Name of Creator: unknown American
- Role Creator: artist
- Format Measurements: JPEG
- Display Materials/Techniques: digital imaging
- Indexing Materials/Techniques:
- Term Materials Techniques: digital imaging
- Display Creation Date: unknown
- Date Qualifier: Date of original
- Earliest Date: unknown
- Latest Date: 1913-02
- Location/Repository Name:
- Type: currentRepository: New Mexico State University Library
- Indexing Subject Term: La Bajada Hill (N.M.); United States Highway 66

- Description/Descriptive Note: Image showing cars traveling a hillside road with multiple switchbacks.
- Inscription: Printed caption on top left reads, "Automobile Road on La Bajada Hill on 'Ocean to Ocean Scenic Highway,' near Santa Fe, New Mexico." Older database indicates the original item is a tinted photomechanical post card.
- Related Work Relationship Type: related to
- Label for Related Work: Ms02230102
- Location of Related Work: New Mexico State University Library
- Related Collection Relationship Type: part of
- Label for Related Collection: Ms0223, Thomas K. Todsen Photographs
- Location of Related Collection: New Mexico State University Library
- Rights for Work: Copyright NMSU Board of Regents

Exercise 5.3
Danzante (matachin) Group

- Object/Work Type: digital image
- Title: Danzante (matachin) group
- Display Creator: unknown
- Name of Creator: unknown
- Role Creator: photographer
- Format Measurements: JPEG
- Display Materials Techniques: digital imaging
- Indexing Materials Techniques:
- Term Materials Techniques: digital imaging
- Display Creation Date: 2009-02-19
- Date Qualifier: Date of original
- Earliest Date: 1907-01-01
- Latest Date: 1907-12-31
- Location/Repository Name:
- Type: currentRepository: New Mexico State University Library
- Indexing Subject Term: Matachines (Dance)
- Description/Descriptive Note: Description in older database reads, "Danzante (matachin) group, man third from right is Cenovio Avalos, second from right is Francisco Dominguez. Las Cruces or Tortugas,

New Mexico," and indicates that the original is a glass negative. Image shows a group composed of men in costume and young girls in white dresses. Digitized using Adobe Photoshop CS3 Macintosh, at 8 bits, 300 dpi

- Related Work Relationship: related to
- Label for Related Work: Ms00040260
- Location of Related Work: New Mexico State University Library, Archives and Special Collections Department, Rio Grande Historical Collections
- Related Collection Relationship Type: part of
- Label for Related Collection: Ms0004 Amador Family Papers
- Location of Related Collection: New Mexico State University Library, Archives and Special Collections Department, Rio Grande Historical Collections
- Rights for Work: Copyright NMSU Board of Regents
- Related Resource Relationship Type: part of larger context
- Label for Related Resource: Rocky Mountain Online Archives, Register of the Amador Family Papers, 1836-1949, *http://rmoa.unm.edu/docviewer.php?docId=nmlcu1ms4.xml*

6

Using VRA Core 4.0

Abstract: This chapter describes the history, development, and use of the Visual Resources Association (VRA) Core 4.0 metadata language, which is especially useful for the description of digital images. The structure of VRA Core and the content standards used with it are discussed, as well as its compatibility with XML. Also considered is how VRA Core is designed to embody the Functional Requirements for Bibliographic Records (FRBR) user tasks and its adherence to the one-to-one principle. The chapter discusses the vocabularies that can be used with VRA Core. Included are detailed descriptions of the elements of VRA Core, and exercises for practising the use of the standard.

Key words: Visual Resources Association, VRA Core, digital images, FRBR tasks, Cultural Objects.

Introduction

Image collections provide the most compelling case for quality metadata. Search and discovery remains predominantly a language-based enterprise, so images need textual surrogates to represent them for these purposes. Ideally, the surrogate will support the FRBR tasks of finding, identifying, selecting, and obtaining; and aid cultural heritage institutions in outreach and interpretation, as well as discovery and retrieval (Elings, 2007, p. 10). A metadata record serves as an image's textual surrogate, and can aid in all these tasks.

At the conceptual level, VRA Core provides a basic element set to consider when designing descriptive metadata fields for a database model (Eklund, 2007, p. 46). The Visual Resources Association created

VRA Core to be a single element set that can be applied as many times as necessary to create records to describe works of visual culture, as well as the images that document them. VRA facilitates the sharing of information among visual resources collections about works and images.

Users of VRA Core are visual resource professionals such as slide librarians, museum librarians, and art historians. The original developers of VRA Core were slide librarians who had surrogates of famous artistic works in their collections, but rarely the original work. While their users might be looking for the Mona Lisa, the slide librarians realized a subtle distinction. What was actually in their collections, what they needed to describe, was an image of the Mona Lisa, rather than the original. The librarians could add a catalog record for the Mona Lisa to their database, but it would be more correct to say that they owned an image of the Mona Lisa. However, at the same time, the users of their libraries needed information about both the original artwork and the surrogate in the slide collection that they would actually use. The visual resources community realized early on that they needed to catalog both the original work and the image held in their collection.

VRA Core closely obeys the one-to-one principle developed by the Dublin Core community (Miller, 2011b, p. 216), which states, "Only one object or resource may be described within a single metadata set" (Visual Resources Association, n.d.a, N. pag.). However, in many cases the image being described does not itself conform to the one-to-one principle. Photographs of museum exhibits often depict the multiple works found in the exhibit. If the exhibit is considered a piece of art in itself, then one photograph may only contain a portion of the whole "work." There may be many images of a single work (how many reproductions of the Mona Lisa must there be?). A building may be considered an important architectural work of art, and perhaps a famous photographer took a photograph of that building – and maybe your textbook has a reproduction of that photograph. All of these works of art and reproductions have complex relationships to each other, and VRA Core attempts to make these relationships clear.

Eklund points out that "Cultural works are as individual as the artists who create them and the scholars who write about them" (2007, p. 45), and that much of the data we have about cultural works comes from scholars, who can vary in opinion on the specifics of a work of art. Therefore, regularizing data about cultural objects can be a significant challenge. The VRA Core aims to be flexible yet provide sufficient structure to accommodate this challenge.

VRA Core 4.0 intentionally aims to address the FRBR User Tasks. These basic tasks are to find, identify, select, and obtain (International Federation of Library Associations, 2009). These tasks are good touchstones for evaluating the success of our metadata. Further, if the purpose of metadata is to make the user successful in these tasks, we can see how consistent, quality metadata creation is vital to images especially, since they don't have inherent descriptive text.

Finding the right image requires that the metadata inform the user that the image potentially conveys the specific work, the subject matter, or relation to a certain entity, like an artist or named collection, that they seek. The metadata must be specific enough for the user to select the best resource among possible candidates within a result set, and the metadata records must be distinct enough to identify the desired resource. Once the user has found, chosen, and identified the resource, successful metadata then facilitates the obtaining of it.

Development of VRA Core

VRA Core has been evolving since the introduction of VRA Core 1.0 in the late 1990s. VRA Core operates with the content standard CCO, and is often used in conjunction with the Getty vocabularies AAT, TGN, and ULAN. For those familiar with library cataloging, think of VRA as MARC (the tags), CCO as AACR2 (the content or semantics), AAT and TGN as the Library of Congress subject headings (the controlled vocabulary), and ULAN as the Library of Congress Name Authority File. VRA Core has been mapped to Dublin Core, so transferring VRA metadata across systems is viable, and the VRA elements have been built in as a metadata scheme option in the popular digital asset management platform CONTENTdm.

Versions 1.0–3.0 started out with an element (or category) set, but no structure or encoding (XML). These elements are (Table 6.1):

While you can see a resemblance to Dublin Core in many of the categories and in its simplicity, you can also see accommodations for unique aspects of art and/or museum objects. The concept of relation to other works addressed a need that was wanting in library cataloging standards for non-serial objects. All the elements in VRA Core 1.0–3.0 are repeatable and can be given in any order (Miller, 2011, p. 216).

VRA Core 4.0 was introduced in 2007. Two primary catalysts inspired the revision of VRA Core 3.0: the VRA-sponsored CCO project and the emergence of XML as the data exchange format of choice (Eklund, 2007,

Table 6.1 **Elements in VRA 1.0–3.0**

Record Type	ID Number
Type	Style/Period
Title	Culture
Measurements	Subject
Material	Relation
Technique	Description
Creator	Source
Date	Rights
Location	

p. 45). The development of CCO gave the community a standard for the content of the data entered into VRA Core, and XML provided a structure for the data and a standardized and highly interoperable means for transferring metadata records. The revision also took into account the growing importance of FRBR in the library community. VRA 4.0 became a standard that addressed more community needs and improved data sharing, yet still was a core standard, able to be adapted to the needs of individual institutions.

There are a few key differences in VRA 4.0 that users of previous versions of VRA Core will notice. The primary difference is the change in structuring element qualifiers. In order to work within the XML encoding structure, the element qualifiers found in previous versions had to be restructured into sub-elements and attributes. The other changes concern the elements themselves. The Record Types "image" and "work" are expanded to include "collection" to further describe how museum collections organize resources. It also changes "Creator" (a term inherited from Dublin Core) and instead uses "Agent" to separate the element from a statement of contribution to the intellectual content of the work (donors can be "agents," but not "creators"). Under the element "agent," a sub-element, "role," specifies the contribution of the named person or entity to the record (Miller, 2011, p. 219). These elements support usage of terms familiar to users of art collections.

VRA Core 4.0 elements

Much of the information in this section is taken from the 2007 article, *Herding Cats: CCO, XML, and the VRA Core*, and the *VRA Core 4.0 Element Description*, both of which were authored by Janice Eklund.

These are excellent resources for learning about the proper usage of VRA Core 4.0, and users should turn to them for detailed information on the intricacies of VRA Core 4.0. The information here aims to give you a foundation to begin working with this element set.

The VRA Core XML schema has 19 elements and 23 sub-elements. Some of these elements and sub-elements have attributes that make the data in an element more specific. VRA Core 4.0 also has nine global attributes that may be applied to any element or sub-element as needed, and two sub-elements called *display* and *notes* that are optional for each element set.

There are two versions of VRA Core 4.0: restricted and unrestricted. In the restricted version, the date formats and the values that can be entered in the *type* attributes are mandated. The standardization of these values allows increased interoperability when data is being aggregated or shared. The unrestricted version allows dates to be entered in any format, and any values can be entered into the *type* attributes.

In the list below, the elements are marked by bold print, the sub-elements are in regular font, and the attributes are in italics. The global attributes are listed below the elements. In addition to the sub-elements listed under each element, one **display** and one **notes** sub-element may be added to any element set as needed. Repeatable elements that allow multiple index values are contained, along with the **display** and **notes** sub-elements, within the *<elementSet></elementSet>* tags (Visual Resources Association, 2007, p. 1).

Elements

- **Work, collection, image (id)**
- **Agent**
  - Attribution
  - Culture
  - Dates *(type)*
    - earliestDate *(circa)*
    - latestDate *(circa)*
  - Name *(type)*
  - Role
- **culturalContext**
- **Date** ***(type)***
  - earliestDate *(circa)*
  - latestDate *(circa)*

- **Description**
- **Inscription**
  - Author
  - Position
  - Text *(type)*
- **Location *(type)***
  - Name *(type)*
  - Refid *(type)*
- **Material *(type)***
- **Measurements *(type, unit)***
- **Relation *(type, relids)***
- **Rights *(type)***
  - rightsHolder
  - text
- **Source**
  - Name *(type)*
  - Refid *(type)*
- **stateEdition (count, num, type)**
  - Description
  - Name
- **stylePeriod**
- **Subject**
  - Term *(type)*
- **Technique**
- **Textref**
  - Name *(type)*
  - Refid *(type)*
- **Title (type)**
- **Worktype**

Global attributes

- dataDate
- extent
- href
- pref

- refid
- rules
- source
- vocab
- xml:lang

Element definitions

Work, collection, or image

The only thing that is required in a VRA Core 4.0 record is an indication of whether the item being described is a work, an image, or a collection. The words work, image, and collection may mean different things to different institutions, but there are very clear definitions for each within the context of VRA Core 4.0:

A **work** is a unique entity such as an object or event. Examples include a painting, sculpture, or photograph; a building or other construction in the built environment; an object of material culture, or a performance. Works may be simple or complex. Works may have component parts that are cataloged as works themselves but related to the larger work in a whole/part or hierarchical fashion via the RELATION element.

An **image** is a visual representation of a work in either whole or part. The representation serves to provide access to the work when the work itself cannot be experienced first-hand. In image collections, such representations typically are found in the form of slides, photographs, and/or digital files.

A **collection** is an aggregate of work or image records. A collection may comprise multiple items that are conceptually or physically arranged together for the purpose of cataloging or retrieval. This record type can also be used to record an archival group that shares a common provenance or a series that encompasses multiple individual titles.

In the XML structure of VRA Core 4.0, this element (work, image, or collection) is considered *the* top level element, because without a resource to describe there is no need for any of the other elements. When a VRA Core 4.0 record is displayed in XML, you can see that all the other descriptive elements are nested within the top level element.

Figure 6.1 **Booth of Casey-Ranch, Roswell Apple Show**

New Mexico State University Library, Archives and Special Collections

```
<work id="i_1823743" refid="04500236">
  <dateSet>
    <display>1911</display>
    <date type="creation">
      <earliestDate>1911</earliestDate>
      <latestDate>1911</latestDate>
    </date>
  </dateSet>
  <locationSet>
    <location type="repository">
      <name type="corporate">New Mexico State University
Rio Grande Historical Collections</name>
    </location>
  </locationSet>
  <titleSet>
    <display> Booth of Casey-Ranch, Roswell Apple Show
</display>
    <title type="descriptive" pref="true" xml:lang=
"en">Booth Casey-Ranch, Roswell Apple Show </title>
```

```
  </titleSet>
 </work>
 <image>
  <dateSet>
  <display>2008-11-21</display>
  <date type="creation">
    <earliestDate>2008-11-21</earliestDate>
    <latestDate>2008-11-21</latestDate>
  </date>
  </dateSet>
    <descriptionSet>
      <description>Created on an Epson Expression 1640XL,
500 ppi, 24 bit</description>
    </descriptionSet>
    <measurementsSet>
      <display>56.28 KB</display>
      <measurements/>
    </measurementsSet>
    <relationSet>
      <relation type="imageOf" refid="04500236"/>
    </relationSet>
    <techniqueSet>
      <display>digital imaging</display>
      <technique/>
    </techniqueSet>
    <titleSet>
      <title>Digitized image from photograph</title>
    </titleSet>
    <worktypeSet>
      <display>digital image</display>
      <worktype/>
    </worktypeSet>
</image>
```

For a more in-depth example of how VRA Core elements nest within the top element, please refer back to the example work and image records in Chapter 2.

While the top level element is the only *required* element of a VRA Core 4.0 record, there is a recommendation for the minimal level of description that a record for a work or an image should have.

Table 6.2 **Recommended element set for minimal description**

Work record	Image record
Worktype	Worktype
Title	Title
Agent	
Location	
Date	

Additionally, all image records must be accompanied by one or more work records, because an image is only a surrogate for the work and cannot stand by itself.

Below are the definitions for each element in VRA Core 4.0. These definitions are broad indications of how the elements should be used. For more detailed instructions about formatting the data, VRA Core 4.0 users generally turn to the content standard CCO, although AACR2 could also be used.

agent
Not required, repeatable

Sub-elements:
  name
    Attribute: type
      Restricted values: *personal, corporate, family, other*
  culture
  dates
    Attribute: type
      Restricted values: *life, activity, other*
    earliestDate
    latestDate
  role
  attribution

Description: The names, appellations, or other identifiers assigned to an individual, group, or corporate body that has contributed to the design, creation, production, manufacture, or alteration of the work or image. When more than one agent is cited, the *extent* attribute may be used to qualify the role sub-element for one or both names. In the case of a named individual, group, or corporate body, the culture sub-element refers to the nationality or culture of the individual, group, or corporate body in the name sub-element. In cases where no identifiable individual, group, or corporate body can be named, creation responsibility is assumed by the culture sub-element. To record the cultural context within which a work, collection, or image was created, independent of the nationality or culture of the creator, use the CULTURAL CONTEXT element (Visual Resources Association, 2007, p. 3). It is recommended that a controlled vocabulary, such as LCNAF or ULAN, be used whenever possible.

culturalContext

Not required, repeatable

Description: The name of the culture, people (ethnonym), or adjectival form of a country name from which a Work, Collection, or Image originates, or the cultural context with which the Work, Collection, or Image has been associated (Visual Resources Association, 2007, p. 6). The use of a controlled vocabulary, such as the ULAN Editorial Guidelines Chapter 4.7 Appendix G, *Nationalities and Places*, AAT, or LCSH is recommended where possible.

date

Not required, repeatable

Attribute: type

Restricted values: alteration, broadcast, bulk, commission, creation, design, destruction, discovery, exhibition, inclusive, performance, publication, restoration, view, other

Sub-elements:

earliestDate

Attribute:circa

Restricted values: true, false

latestDate

Attribute: circa

Restricted values: true, false

Description: Date or range of dates associated with the creation, design, production, presentation, performance, construction, or alteration, etc. of the work or image. Dates may be expressed as free text or numerical. The Boolean *circa* attribute may be added to either sub-element to indicate an approximate date. For image records, the date element refers to the view date, if known (Visual Resources Association, 2007, p. 7). It is recommended that values be entered according to ISO 8601 standards for data content (*http://www.cl.cam.ac.uk/~mgk25/iso-time.html*), i.e. YYYY, YYYY-MM, or

YYYY-MM-DD. Dates before the Common Era (BCE or BC) should be entered with a minus sign (-) in the form –YYYY, whenever possible.

description

Not required, repeatable

Description: A free-text note about the Work, Collection, or Image, including comments, description, or interpretation, that gives additional information not recorded in other categories. For element-specific notes, use the optional **notes** sub-element (Visual Resources Association, 2007, p. 10).

inscription

Not required, repeatable

Sub-elements:

author

position

text

Attribute: type

Restricted values: signature, mark, caption, date, text, translation, other

Description: All marks or written words added to the object at the time of production or in its subsequent history, including signatures, dates, dedications, texts, and colophons, as well as marks, such as the stamps of silversmiths, publishers, or printers. The location of this text or symbol may be specified by the position sub-element. If a translation of the text into the language of the catalog record is also provided, include in a repeated element with the text type of *translation* (Visual Resources Association, 2007, p. 11).

location

Not required, repeatable

Attribute: type

Restricted values: creation, discovery, exhibition, formerOwner, formerRepository, formerSite, installation, intended, other, owner, performance, publication, repository, site

Sub-elements:

name

Attribute: type

Restricted values: corporate, geographic, other, personal

refid

Attribute: type

Restricted values: accession, barcode, shelfList, other

Description: The geographic location and/or name of the repository, building, site, or other entity whose boundaries include the Work or Image. Inclusion of a *type* attribute distinguishes between different kinds of locations, e.g. repository locations, creation locations, discovery locations, etc. The optional *extent* attribute may also be used here to further specify or disambiguate geographic term types. Note that repository id numbers (museum or private collection accession or inventory numbers), formerly contained in the Core 3 ID Number element, are here mapped to the Location **refid** sub-element. Inclusion of these alphanumeric strings that pinpoint a particular work within a particular location serves to disambiguate identically titled works by the same artist held by the same repository (e.g. Raphael, "Madonna and Child.") Repeatable sub-elements allow the inclusion of multiple museum inventory numbers if an object id number has changed over time. For id numbers that are independent of repository, such as *catalog raisonné* numbers, use the **TEXTREF** element (Visual Resources Association, 2007, p. 14). It is recommended that a controlled vocabulary such as TGN, the BHA Index, the *Grove Dictionary of Art* Location Appendix, or LCSH is used whenever possible.

material

Not required, repeatable

Description: The substance of which a work or an image is composed (Visual Resources Association, 2007, p. 18). The use of a controlled vocabulary such as AAT is recommended when possible.

measurement

Not required, repeatable

Attribute: type

Restricted values: area, base, bit-depth, circumference, count, depth, diameter, distanceBetween, duration, fileSize, height, length, resolution, runningTime, scale, size, target, weight, width, other

Attribute: unit

Restricted values: Refer to ISO standard for units and measures: *http://ts.nist.gov/WeightsAndMeasures/Publications/appxc.cfm.* Values should follow standard 2-letter abbreviations without punctuation (Example: cm)

Description: The physical size, shape, scale, dimensions, or format of the Work or Image. Dimensions may include such measurements as volume, weight, area, or running time. If the measurements do not describe the entire work or image, use the extent attribute to specify the part of the work being measured. The unit used in the measurement must be specified (Visual Resources Association, 2007, p. 19).

relation

Not required, repeatable

Attribute: type

Restricted values: see table below

Attribute: relid

Restricted values: links the XML record to the related work or collection XML record(s) *id* attribute

Description: Terms or phrases describing the identity of the related work and the relationship between the work being cataloged and the related work or image. Use this element to relate work records to other work or collection records, or image records to work or collection records. If full relational reciprocity is not explicitly recorded in a local database (e.g. only the part to whole relationship is recorded, and not whole to part), it is recommended that the data exporter add the reciprocal value, based on a controlled set of terms (see Table 6.3).

rights

Not required, repeatable

Attributes: type

Restricted values: copyrighted, publicDomain, undetermined, other

Sub-elements:

rightsHolder

text

Description: Information about the copyright status and the rights holder for a work, collection, or image. The optional notes sub-element may include justifications, conditions, or restraints on use, contact or licensing information, or other intellectual property statements as may be desired. The global *href* attribute may be used to hold a hypertext link to a website containing rights and/or contact information (Visual Resources Association, 2007, p. 25).

Table 6.3 Restricted values for the **relation** element

Relationship Type	Reciprocal Relationship Type
<general – default>	
relatedTo	relatedTo
<hierarchical – group/collection/series to parts>	
partOf	largerContextFor
formerlyPartOf	formerlyLargerContextFor
<a work and its components>	
componentOf	componentIs
partnerInSetWith	partnerInSetWith
<works that are related as steps in the creation process>	
preparatoryFor	basedOn
studyFor	studyIs
cartoonFor	cartoonIs
modelFor	modelIs
planFor	planIs
counterProofFor	counterProofIs
printingPlateFor	printingPlateIs
reliefFor	impressionIs
prototypeFor	prototypeIs
<works designed to be displayed together>	
designedFor	contextIs
mateOf	mateOf
partnerInSetWith	partnerInSetWith
pendantOf	pendantOf
exhibitedAt	venueFor
<works copied after or depicting other works>	
copyAfter	copyIs
depicts	depictedIn
derivedFrom	sourceFor
facsimileOf	facsimileIs
replicaOf	replicaIs
versionOf	versionIs
<work to image relationships>	
imageOf	imageIs

Source: Visual Resources Association, 2007, p. 24.

Use of the Modern Language Association (MLA) rules for bibliographic citation for print sources is recommended when necessary.

source

Not required, repeatable

Sub-elements:

name:

Attributes: type

Restricted values: book, donor, electronic, serial, vendor, other

refid:

Attributes: type

Restricted values: citation, ISBN, ISSN, openURL, URI, vendor, other

Description: A reference to the source of the information recorded about the work or the image. For a work record, this may be a citation to the sole source of the information recorded in a catalog record. For an image, it may be used to provide information about the supplying agency, vendor, or individual. In the case of copy photography, it can be used to record a bibliographic citation or other description of the image source. In all cases, names and source identification numbers may be included. If all information recorded about a work, image, or collection comes from a single source, it should be recorded here. However, each individual element of the Core may include a *source* attribute to reflect an information source pertaining specifically to that element within a work, image, or collection (Visual Resources Association, 2007, p. 26). MLA rules for bibliographic citation recommended when necessary.

stateEdition

Not required, repeatable

Attribute: type (state, edition, or impression)

Restricted values: state, edition, impression, other

Attribute: num (state number or edition number)

Attribute: count (number of known states, known editions, or number of impression in an edition)

Sub-elements:

name

description

Description: The identifying number and/or name assigned to the state or edition of a work that exists in more than one form and the placement of that work in the context of prior or later issuances of multiples of the same work. For published volumes, such as books, portfolios, series, or sets, the edition is usually expressed as a number in relation to other editions printed. In other cases, a scholar may have identified a series of editions, which have then been numbered sequentially. A state or edition may also be identified by a name or phrase. If the data is derived from a secondary source, such as a *catalog raisonné*, it should be included in a source attribute (Visual Resources Association, 2007, p. 27).

stylePeriod

Not required, repeatable

Description: The identifying number and/or name assigned to the state or edition of a work that exists in more than one form and the placement of that work in the context of prior or later issuances of multiples of the same work. For published volumes, such as books, portfolios, series, or sets, the edition is usually expressed as a number in relation to other editions printed. In other cases, a scholar may have identified a series of editions, which have then been numbered sequentially. A state or edition may also be identified by a name or phrase. If the data is derived from a secondary source, such as a *catalog raisonné*, it should be included in a source attribute (Visual Resources Association, 2007, p. 29). Use of a controlled vocabulary such as AAT is recommended when possible.

subject

Not required, repeatable

Sub-elements:

Term

Attribute: type

Restricted values:

For names: corporateName, familyName, otherName, personalName, scientificName

For locations: builtworkPlace, geographicPlace, otherPlace

For descriptive, narrative, or thematic content: conceptTopic, descriptiveTopic, iconographicTopic, otherTopic

Description: Terms or phrases that describe, identify, or interpret the Work or Image and what it depicts or expresses. These may include generic terms that describe the work and the elements that it comprises, terms that identify particular people, geographic places, narrative and iconographic themes, or terms that refer to broader concepts or interpretations. Use of a Subject Authority, from which these data values may be derived, is recommended. The global *source* attribute may be used to isolate local collection or user-supplied terminology that is not controlled by any authority (Visual Resources Association, 2007, p. 30). The use of a controlled vocabulary such as AAT, TGN, TGM, Iconclass, LCSH, LCNAF, or the Sears Subject Headings is recommended when possible.

technique

Not required, repeatable

Description: The production or manufacturing processes, techniques, and methods incorporated in the fabrication or alteration of the work or image (Visual Resources Association, 2007, p. 32).

textref

Not required, repeatable

Sub-elements:

name

Attribute: type

Restricted values: book, catalog, corpus, electronic, serial, other

refid

Attribute: type

Restricted values: citation, openURL, ISBN, ISSN, URI, vendor, other

Description: Contains the name of a related textual reference and any type of unique identifier that text assigns to a Work or Collection that is independent of any repository. **Refid** examples include exhibition and *catalog raisonné* numbers, or identification numbers assigned to works of art in the scholarly literature that are commonly included in scholarly discussion to further identify a work, such as Bartsch or Beazley numbers. The global *source* attribute may be used to cite a scholarly source from which the number was derived, if the unique identifier was not recorded from the primary source cited in the name sub-element. The global *href* attribute may be used to contain an actionable hypertext reference to an online source for the cited text or reference identifier (Visual Resources Association, 2007, p. 33).

title

Not required, repeatable

Attribute: type

Restricted values:

For work title: brandName, cited, creator, descriptive, former, inscribed, owner, popular, repository, translated, other

For image title: generalView, partialView

Description: Contains the name of a related textual reference and any type of unique identifier that text assigns to a Work or Collection that is independent of any repository. **Refid** examples include exhibition and *catalog raisonné* numbers, or identification numbers assigned to works of art in the scholarly literature that are commonly included in scholarly discussion to further identify a work, such as Bartsch or Beazley numbers. The global *source* attribute may be used to cite a scholarly source from which the number was derived, if the unique identifier was not recorded from the primary source cited in the name sub-element. The global *href* attribute may be used to contain an actionable hypertext reference to an online source for the cited text or reference identifier (Visual Resources Association, 2007, p. 35).

work type

Not required, repeatable

Definition: Identifies the specific type of WORK, COLLECTION, or IMAGE being described in the record (Visual Resources Association, 2007, p. 37).

While **work type** has no restricted values, it is recommended that terms from AAT be used for **work** and **collection type**, and that the following terms from AAT are used for **image type:** black-and-white transparency, color transparency (for slides or positive transparencies), black-and-white negative, color negative (for negative transparencies), photographic print (for photographic prints), or digital image.

Global attributes definitions

Global attributes are optional and may be added to any element or sub-element as needed. Definitions are as follows:

- *dataDate* refers to the date and/or time a particular piece of data was entered.
- *extent* refers to the part of the work, image or collection being described by the element or sub-element that it modifies.
- *href* refers to a hypertext reference that provides a link to another electronic resource.
- *pref* indicates that a particular data value is the preferred value when multiple data values for the same element or sub-element exist.
- *refid* refers to id numbers or codes coming from the local institution or resource named in the *source* attribute.
- *rules* refers to any data content standards used to construct the value recorded in the element (e.g. AACR2, CCO).
- *source* refers to the local, print, or electronic source from which information is derived for a specific element (e.g. Grove Dictionary of Art). Please note: SOURCE is also used as an element and should be used when you want to record a single print or electronic source for information pertaining to the entire record rather than pertaining to individual elements.
- *vocab* refers to the controlled vocabulary source from which the term or phrase is recorded (e.g. AAT, LCSH).
- *xml:lang* refers to the language in which the information is recorded in the system (e.g. English, French) (Visual Resources Association, 2007, p. 1).

Another option for museum and art collection professionals is the CDWA, a product of the AITF, which encouraged dialog between art historians, art repositories, and information providers so that together they could develop guidelines for describing works of art, architecture, groups of objects, and visual and textual surrogates (see Chapter 5).

Example record

See Figure 6.2.

Figure 6.2 Taos Indian Pueblo, New Mexico

New Mexico State University Library, Archives and Special Collections

Available information:

- Digitized: September 3, 2003, using Adobe Photoshop CS4 Macintosh, at 8 bits and 300 dpi. Digital image identified by the string "02231282"
- Description: Verso: Taos Indian Pueblo, New Mexico
- Location: Taos, New Mexico
- Date: 30 July 1940 (postmark)
- Photographer's number: 45
- Notes: Distributed and copyrighted by J. R. Willis, Box 665, Albuquerque, New Mexico. Genuine Curteich-Chicago 'C. T. Art-Colortone' Post Card
- Collection Number: Ms0223
- Collection Name: Thomas K. Todsen Photographs
- Physical Description: photocopy and copy negative
- Work refid="Ms02231282"
- Agent type="other": unknown
- Agent:
- Culture: American
- Cultural Context: American

- Date:
- Latest Date circa="true":1940
- Description: Image of a pueblo in front of a large hill or mountain. Older database indicates that the verso of the image states that it is a Taos Indian Pueblo in New Mexico, that the item is "Distributed and copyrighted by J. R. Willis, Box 665, Albuquerque, New Mexico," and that it is a "Genuine Curteich-Chicago 'C. T. Art-Colortone' Post Card."
- Location:
- Name type="geographic": Taos (N.M.)
- Location type="repository": New Mexico State University Libraries (Las Cruces, New Mexico, United States)
- Material vocab="AAT": Photographic prints
- Relation type="PartOf": Thomas K. Todsen Photograph Collection
- Relation relid="Ms 0223"
- Rights type="copyrighted": Copyright NMSU Board of Regents, Please send questions to archives@lib.nmsu.edu
- Subject vocab="LCSH" type="Geographic Place": Taos (N.M.)
- Subject vocab="LCSH" type="Descriptive Topic": Pueblo architecture
- Title: Taos Indian Pueblo, New Mexico
- Work type: Photographic Prints
- Image refid="02231282"
- Date type="creation": 2003-09-03
- Description: Digitized using Adobe Photoshop CS4 Macintosh, at 8 bits and 300 dpi
- Relation type="Image of": Ms02231282
- Technique: Digital imaging
- Title: Digitized image from photograph
- Work type: Digital image

Exercises

Each of the following exercises presents a surrogate of an original work (Figure 6.1, 6.3 and 6.4), held by the New Mexico State University Library, along with the information available to the metadata cataloger.

Each image should have an accompanying work and image record. The last exercise may have more than one work record associated with the image record.

Exercise 6.1: Unrestricted VRA Core 4.0

Available information (from a Dublin Core description of the digital image):

- Title: Booth of Casey-Ranch, Roswell Apple Show
- Subject: Agricultural exhibitions, Farm produce, Casey Ranch
- Description: Handwritten captions on image read "Booth of Casey-Ranch" and "Winner of 5-Blue-Ribbons, 1 Second + Diploma, Roswell Apple Show. Oct, 5, 6, 7, 1911, copyright 1912 by L.W. Adams." Image shows a decorative produce display showcasing a variety of produce. Much of the produce is displayed in arranged crates. Identification signs among the crates read "Bellflower", "Vandi Ver Pippin", "R.I. Greening", "Keiffer Pears", "Apple-Commerce", "Gano", and "Blacktwig."
- Publisher: New Mexico State University Library
- Date Original: 1911-10-05 – 07
- Date Digital: 2004-01-13
- Type: Still Image
- Format: image/jpeg
- Digitization Specifications: 24 bits, 200 dpi
- Identifier: Ms04500236
- Source: UA0450, mounted photographic print
- Collection: University Archives: Fabian Garcia Papers
- Rights: Copyright, NMSU Board of Regents. Please send questions to: archives@lib.nmsu.edu

Exercise 6.2: Restricted VRA Core

Figure 6.3 **Cliff dwellings west of Santa Fe, New Mexico**

New Mexico State University Library, Archives and Special Collections

Available information:

- Handwritten caption on item reads "Cliff dwelling west of Santa Fe, N.M., 1923"
- Original image is part of the Leslie K. Goforth Photograph Collection
- The digital image is identified by the string Ms0194016
- Older database indicates that the original was a black and white photographic print

Exercise 6.3: Work within work

Available information:

- Caption on front reads: "La Fonda, the Harvey Hotel at Santa Fe. After painting by Fred Geary"

Figure 6.4 La Fonda, the Harvey Hotel at Santa Fe, New Mexico

New Mexico State University Library, Archives and Special Collections

- Original image is part of the Thomas K. Todsen Photograph Collection
- The digital copy of the image is identified by the string Ms02230353
- An older database indicates the original is a photomechanical color post card

Answer key

Exercise 6.1
Booth of Casey-Ranch, Roswell Apple Show

- Work refid=Ms04500236
- Agent: unknown (American)
- Cultural context: American
- Date: 1911-10
- Description: Image of a decorative produce display at the Roswell Apple Show. Display contains arranged crates showcasing a number of different types of apples. Identification signs among the crates read “Bellflower”, “Vandi Ver Pippin”, “R.I. Greening”, “Keiffer Pears”, “Apple-Commerce”, “Gano”, and “Blacktwig.”
- Inscription:
  - Position: Bottom left
  - Text: Booth of Casey-Ranch

- Inscription:
  - Position: Bottom right
  - Text: Winner of 5-Blue-Ribbons, 1 Second + Diploma, Roswell Apple Show. Oct, 5, 6, 7, 1911, copyright 1912 by L.W. Adams.
- Location type="repository": New Mexico State University Libraries (Las Cruces, New Mexico, United States)
- Location type:
  - Geographic: Roswell (N.M.)
- Material: Photographic prints
- Relation:
  - Depicts: Booth of Casey Ranch, Roswell Apple show
  - Version Is: 04500236
- Rights type="copyrighted": Copyright NMSU Board of Regents, Please send questions to archives@lib.nmsu.edu
- Subject:
  - Corporate Name: Casey Ranch
  - Other Name: Roswell Apple Show
  - Descriptive Topic: Agricultural exhibitions
  - Descriptive Topic: Farm produce
- Title: Booth of Casey Ranch, Roswell Apple Show
- Work Type: Photographic Prints

- Image refid="04500236"
- Date type="creation": 2004-01-13
- Description: Digitized at 24 bits and 200 dpi
- Relation:
  - Image of: Ms04500236
- Title: Digitized image black and white photograph
- Work type: Digital image

Exercise 6.2
Cliff dwellings west of Santa Fe, New Mexico

- Work refid="Ms01940162"
- Agent type="other": unknown

- Agent:
  - Culture: American
- Cultural Context: American
- Date type="creation": 1923
- Description: Photographic print of cliff dwellings west of Santa Fe, New Mexico.
- Inscription:
  - Position: Bottom
  - Text type="caption": Cliff dwelling west of Santa Fe, N.M., 1923
- Location type="repository"
  - Name type="corporate": New Mexico State University Libraries (Las Cruces, New Mexico, United States)
- Location type="site"
  - Name type="geographic": Santa Fe (N.M.)
- Relation type="Part Of": Leslie K. Goforth Photograph Collection
- Relation type="relid": Ms 0194
- Rights type="copyrighted": Copyright NMSU Board of Regents, Please send questions to archives@lib.nmsu.edu
- Subject:
  - Term type="Descriptive Topic" vocab="LCSH": Cliff-dwellings
  - Term type="Geographic Place" vocab="LCSH": Santa Fe, New Mexico
- Technique: photography
- Title: Cliff dwellings west of Santa Fe, N.M.
- Work type: photographs

- Image refid="01940162"
- Relation:
  - Image of: Ms01940162
- Title: Digitized image black and white photograph
- Work type: Digital image

Exercise 6.3
La Fonda, the Harvey Hotel at Santa Fe, New Mexico

- Work

- Agent: unknown
- Cultural Context: American
- Date type="creation": 1922
- Description: The La Fonda Hotel is located on the Plaza in Santa Fe, New Mexico, on what has been called the oldest hotel corner in America.
- Location type="site" vocab="LCSH":
  - Geographic Name: Santa Fe, (N.M.)
- Subject vocab="LCSH":
  - Corporate Name: La Fonda Hotel
- Descriptive Topic: Hotels—United States
- Subject vocab="AAT":
  - Descriptive Topic: hotels (public accommodations)

- Work refid="02230353"
- Agent type="personal": Geary, Fred
- Agent:
  - Culture: American
- Cultural Context: American
- Date type="creation":
  - Earliest Date circa="true": 1920
  - Latest Date circa="true": 1940
- Description: Photomechanical color postcard showing a painting by Fred Geary of the La Fonda Hotel from a nearby intersection
- Inscription:
  - Position: Bottom
  - Text type="caption": H-3977 La Fonda, the Harvey Hotel at Santa Fe, New Mexico. After painting by Fred Geary
- Location type="repository":
- Name type="corporate": New Mexico State University Libraries (Las Cruces, New Mexico, United States)
- Relation:
  - Part Of: Thomas K. Todsen Photograph Collection
  - Relid: Ms 0223

- Rights type="copyrighted": Copyright NMSU Board of Regents, Please send questions to archives@lib.nmsu.edu
- Subject:
  - Corporate Name: La Fonda Hotel
  - Corporate Name: Harvey Hotels
  - Geographic Place: Santa Fe, New Mexico
- Technique: Photomechanical processes
- Title: La Fonda, the Harvey Hotel at Santa Fe
- Work type: Photomechanical prints

- Image
- Relation:
  - Image of: 02230353
- Title: Digitized image from photomechanical postcard
- Work type: Digital image

7

The big picture

Abstract: This chapter provides an overview of how metadata produced at a local institution can be shared with metadata created at another institution. Creating shareable metadata and opening your metadata to other services will bring new visitors to your site and increase awareness of your collections. All metadata should be created with shareability in mind, and this chapter will provide ideas for how to make metadata more interoperable. Additionally, this chapter will cover the basics of the Semantic Web and will explain how cultural heritage resources can be described in RDF. Topics include sharing metadata through metasearch, the Semantic Web and RDF, crosswalking and mapping, and OAI-PMH.

Key words: interoperability, shareability, crosswalking, mapping, Semantic Web, RDF, OAI-PMH.

Introduction

The previous chapters explained how to make metadata at your own institution, and how to fill the needs of your own patrons. However, we haven't yet discussed how all of the metadata created at your institution can fit with metadata created at a different institution. From a user's point of view, each metadata record is like a piece of a jigsaw puzzle in their search for resources relevant to their work. How all these records fit together will determine the big picture of resources available for their research topic.

If a researcher is studying a specific topic, he or she needs to know that your institution may own a collection that is relevant to their topic. Previously, unless this collection was well advertised, the researcher may not know that it existed. However, now that you've invested resources into describing your collection, it's equally important to make sure that access to the collection is available through subject portals and aggregations.

Digital collections exist at many institutions and users are no longer geographically limited to collections in their surrounding areas. Users can explore collections held far away as long as the resource has been digitized, and the user is able to find the resource. But how can the user find a resource in your collection if they don't know that the collection exists? The solution is to share metadata about your resources in as many places as possible.

Why should we share our metadata? Increased exposure of our resources' metadata increases exposure of our collections. Providing access to our resources in a variety of portals helps to ensure that researchers looking for resources are able to find them. If a researcher finds an item in our collection, and had not realized that our collection was relevant to their research, they are more likely to think of us in the future. Use of our digital resources broadens our user base and helps our institution remain relevant in the future.

Users familiar with Google and other portals many times completely bypass the "front" webpage to our collection. If a resource in our collection is relevant to their search, they're likely to jump into the collection at that page, and start exploring our resources. But, in order for the first page they see in the collection to make sense, the item needs good metadata to help contextualize the resource and direct the user to other related items.

Shareability

Libraries have developed methods to share metadata with subject portals and national and international portals. An example of this type of portal is OCLC's OAIster (pronounced 'oyster') (*http://oaister.worldcat.org/*). OAIster collects millions of metadata records created by various cultural heritage institutions, allowing users to search across all resources simultaneously. These records are brought together through use of OAI-PMH into a single database.

OAI-PMH divides the world into data providers and service providers. Data providers create and expose their metadata. Service providers collect the metadata, normalize it so that it matches metadata from other harvested collections, and make it searchable through a portal. Although metadata records are only as current as the most recent harvest, OAI-PMH makes refreshing of harvested records fairly simple. Advantages are that the aggregator has control of the database and servers and of results displays, and records can be ranked according to relevance. More details on this protocol follow later in the chapter.

Another common method used to make metadata searchable is metasearch. A specific type of metasearch is NISO Z39.50. The metasearch method performs a live search across multiple databases simultaneously, and returns the results to the users. This is a common approach to simultaneous searching of many databases that libraries subscribe to without having direct access to the metadata. Drawbacks are that searches are processed at the hosts' database, and the library doesn't have control over how results are returned. Another drawback is that results aren't integrated across databases, and there is no way to determine relevance between two different result sets. Advantages are that metadata is up-to-date, and the library does not need to maintain a large database of metadata records.

The semantic web

Another way that libraries can share data with the world is through the Semantic Web and linked data. Current descriptive metadata practices rely on computers transmitting the data and humans reading and understanding the data. However, the Semantic Web aims to make the data understandable by computers so that machines are able to interpret resources and find connections that humans might not be able to, due to the limitations of human understandable metadata. One of the main structures of the Semantic Web is RDF and its use of statements. In this framework, a resource is described using several statements instead of a single metadata record. An RDF statement has three parts, or a "triple." These three parts are subject-predicate-object expressions. Related to the cultural heritage digital collection metadata we've been using in this workbook, the subject is the resource being described (e.g. this book), the predicate is the metadata property (e.g. "creator"), and the object is the metadata string (e.g. "Jackson"). All three parts of this statement can be represented by a uniform resource identifier (URI), and the predicate is drawn from a controlled vocabulary. Ideally, the object is also from a controlled vocabulary.

A visual representation of RDF looks like Figure 7.1:

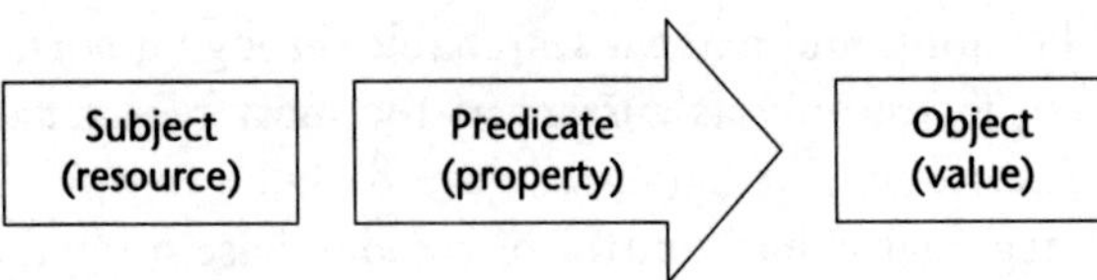

Figure 7.1 RDF Triple

For an example, let's look at the following image (Figure 7.2) and associated metadata:

Title: Wright's Trading Post, Albuquerque, New Mexico
Identifier: 02231177
Type: Image
Format: Image/tiff
Description: Postcard of Wright's Trading Post in Albuquerque, New Mexico
Publisher: New Mexico State University Library

Using RDF triples, we can express the title and type like this:

"02231177" has title "Wright's Trading Post, Albuquerque, New Mexico"
"02231177" has type "image"

Figure 7.2 Wright's Trading Post, Albuquerque, New Mexico

New Mexico State University Library, Archives and Special Collections

In these examples, the subject is the image, defined by a URI (02231177), the predicate is the property name (title or type), and the object is the value of the property ("Wright's Trading Post, Albuquerque, NM," or "image"). See the following exercise (Figure 7.3).

RDF Exercises

Figure 7.3 **Cliff dwellings west of Santa Fe, New Mexico**

New Mexico State University Library, Archives and Special Collections

Title: Cliff dwellings west of Santa Fe, New Mexico
Date: 1923
Type: Image
Format: Image/tiff
Description: Postcard of Cliff dwellings west of Santa Fe, New Mexico
Publisher: New Mexico State University Libraries

01940162 has _____ 1923

________ has title ________

________ has ________ ________

________ has ________ ________

RDF becomes machine readable when it's encoded in XML syntax. However, XML is not the only option for making RDF machine readable.

Because this workbook has addressed XML, we'll show an RDF example encoded in XML. The example below says that "Amy Jackson" (subject) has colleague (predicate) "Rebecca Lubas" (object).

```
<Description about="some.uri/person/amy_jackson">
  <hasColleague resource="some.uri/person/rebecca_lubas"/>
</Description>
```

When RDF is stored in a database, queries can be performed using SPARQL (pronounced "sparkle"), a query language for retrieving and manipulating data stored in RDF. In the semantic web, RDF can be used with OWL (Web Ontology Language). An ontology is a representation of knowledge within a domain through a specific set of concepts and their relationship to each other. OWL is a specific computer language for making ontological statements that can be used with RDF.

RDF is a very powerful language for machines, and allows machines to "understand" the metadata used to describe resources. However, as you can see, it's also very complex and time consuming to identify all resources at this level. The Semantic Web and linked data are still under development as a proof of concept, and may or may not become major future developments of the World Wide Web. Efforts such as those by the Dublin Core Metadata Initiative/Resource Description and Access Task Group may aid in this development by creating RDF vocabularies that will be adopted by the library and other metadata communities (Hillmann et al., 2010). Professionals working in small cultural heritage institutions do not currently need to be overly concerned with the Semantic Web, but should be aware of how metadata is used in this environment and watch its development.

Making records shareable

In order for metadata to be optimized for these types of "big picture" sharing activities, records should be created with sharing in mind.

All descriptive metadata will eventually be seen by humans interested in resources, so human understandability is important. A metadata record should clearly explain the resource being described. Additionally, although your targeted user group may be subject specialists, when your records are exported to an aggregator, the user of a service provider's portal may not be a subject expert. You should ensure that non-subject specialists can also understand the record.

Shreeves et al. (2006) provide the following "six C's and lots of S's of sharable metadata." The "C's" are: context, consistency, coherence, content, communication, and conformance to standards. The number of standards involved are the "lots of S's."

In an aggregated environment, the *context* your individual records may have received from being part of a larger collection is lost to a user. In order to make metadata records shareable, you should provide some contextual information in the metadata. An example of this was articulated by Robin Wendler as the "on a horse" problem (Wendler, 2004). Wendler was working with metadata records from the Theodore Roosevelt collection, and noticed that some records describing images of Roosevelt did not contain the word "Roosevelt." A particular image of Roosevelt sitting on a horse was titled "on a horse," but the record did not contain his name. Since the original record was part of the Roosevelt collection, the metadata creator assumed that the users would know that the image was of Roosevelt. However, in the aggregated environment, there are no clues as to where the record came from, and the record needs to explicitly say that the image is of Theodore Roosevelt.

Metadata from individual repositories should be created with *consistency* in mind. If all records are created with the same practices, an aggregator can make uniform changes across all harvested records to match practices in their own environment. For example, if an aggregator prefers the first name first in the author field, but you've created all of your records with the last name first, the aggregator can flip the order of the name on all records. However, if your practices haven't been consistent and some records have first name first while others have last name first, it will be much more difficult for the aggregator to make all of your records conform to their practices. Important things to remember when trying to make records consistent are to use all fields consistently, use controlled vocabulary consistently, and use consistent encoding schemas. For example, you should choose a controlled vocabulary like LCSH or AAT and use this vocabulary for all metadata records. A common understanding of all fields is important, so that all records are using a field in the same way. This is why standards, such as Dublin Core, VRA Core, EAD, or CDWA, are so important in this community. If one collection uses the "source" field to describe the original resource, and another collection incorrectly uses it to describe the collection, users will not be searching the same information when they limit their search to a specific field. It's also important to consistently use all appropriate fields. If your collection doesn't use a relevant field to describe resources, but the users limit a search to that field, not all resources in your collection may be included in the results.

Metadata records should be able to stand alone and be *coherent* to a non-specialist. As soon as a metadata record leaves your local environment, you cannot assume that users will have any specialized knowledge of the subject. For example, a local battle may be well known to an historic society's community, but a person on the other side of the country may not know anything about it. When creating a metadata record that mentions the battle, be sure to give extra information for individuals who may not know anything about it. As the linked data environment becomes more mature through consistent use of URIs, the data behind the URI will provide this extra information.

The *content* of a metadata record needs to be optimized for sharing. Granularity of the description is an important part of the content, and should be considered before exporting records. For example, in an image collection, most institutions take the time to describe every image. However, individual books are a collection of images held together with structural metadata, and each page could have an associated metadata record. If every page's metadata record was exported to an aggregator, there would be lots of extraneous metadata records. The aggregator will probably only be interested in metadata at the top level of the book, unless the individual pages hold significant information. Metadata creators should also ensure that metadata relevant at only a local level is not exported to a service provider. Many times, this type of metadata is called administrative metadata, and contains information about local digitization equipment and practices, when the resource was digitized, and other information. Although this metadata may be valuable at a local level, it also creates lots of noise in the aggregated environment. Another important aspect of content is awareness of the influence of controlled vocabulary in the aggregated environment. Even though your collection may be using a controlled vocabulary, as soon as metadata leaves your environment and co-mingles with other metadata records, there is no longer a controlled vocabulary for all records. For example, if collection X uses LCSH for subjects, but collection Y uses AAT for subjects, when the records are mixed in an aggregated portal, the benefits of a single controlled vocabulary will be lost. Subject terms from multiple thesauri will be searchable by users. As linked data becomes more common, URIs identifying the controlled vocabulary will travel with the record, and aggregators will be able to identify the multiple controlled vocabularies in their portals.

Finally, *communicating* with service providers is an essential step in the sharing process. This can be as simple as posting your metadata best practices, use of controlled vocabularies, and encoding standards on your website so that service providers can understand how your records are created. If this is documented and accessible, they can easily make changes to optimize your metadata for the highest level of interoperability within their portal.

Sharing records also requires that your institution follows and *conforms* to national *standards* so that aggregators have access to, and can understand, your records. Data structure, data content, controlled vocabularies, and technical standards for encoding and transmitting are essential parts of interoperable metadata.

Appropriate data structure ensures that all repositories are using commonly understood fields and field definitions. Examples of data structure include Dublin Core, MARC and MARCXML, EAD, VRA Core 4.0, and CDWA. Data content standards ensure that all text strings are created consistently across multiple repositories. Examples include AACR2, CCO, and DACS. Controlled vocabulary and encoding standards are helpful to ensure consistency within your own collection, but, as mentioned above, controlled vocabulary may lose significance in an aggregated environment. Examples of controlled vocabulary include LCSH, AAT, LCNAF, and Dublin Core type vocabulary. Encoding standards include ISO 8601 (YYYY-MM-DD) for encoding dates, and ISO 639-2 (three-letter codes) for encoding languages.

Technical standards ensure that metadata can be transmitted and that machines can understand certain fields for optimum indexing. Examples of technical standards include XML, OAI-PMH, and date encoding standards.

Steven Miller identifies five ways to improve metadata interoperability (Miller, 2011, p. 245):

- Use Dublin Core and other standard elements correctly.
- Include sufficient contextual information and access points.
- Enter data values that are machine-processable and linkable.
- Distinguish administrative and technical metadata from descriptive metadata.
- Document your local practices.

How are the following records not optimized for sharing?

title: [Chimpanzee with offspring]
title: [Chimpanzee with infant]
creator: Garst, Genevieve Sherwin, 1922-
creator: Garst, Warren, 1922-
description: Access, 600X480 pixels 72 dpi JPEG, file size ~100 KB to 300 KB depending on JPEG compression and original image size
description: Archive, 24-bit color 1200 dpi TIFF, file size ~6 MB
description: Biomes: forest
description: Class: Mammalia
description: Diet: omnivore
description: Family: Pongidae
description: Geographical continent: Africa
description: Geographical regional: Western Africa, Central Africa
description: Hewlett Packard PS20 Scanner, HP PhotoSmart S20 Scanning Software and default HP S20 color target, Adobe Photoshop 5.5
description: Order: Primates
description: Thumbnail, 150X90 pixels 72 dpi JPEG, file size ~15 KB to 30 KB depending on JPEG compression and original image size
subject: Pan troglodytes
subject: monkey
subject: Chimpanzee
subject: ape
publisher: X State University Libraries
date: 1976–10
date: 2001–01
date: 2001–09
format: Any machine capable of running graphical web browsers, 640X480 minimum monitor resolution
type: image
identifier: *http://xstate.edu/identifier*
relation: Heritage
relation: Warren and Genevieve Garst Photographic Collection
source: G00426
source: Warren and Genevieve Garst Photographic Collection slide no. G0426
title: Recess Time at Grade School

creator: Russell Lee
description: Hobbs, New Mexico. March 1940. "Recess time at grade school in this oil boom town."
date: March 1940
format: image/ jpeg
type: image
identifier: *http://econtent.unm.edu/u?/fmp,284*

Mapping and crosswalking

In your local institution, you might create local metadata fields, or have legacy records created with metadata fields specific to your institution and/or project. While this is appropriate in a local context, you will need to turn these records into metadata records following a common standard, such as Dublin Core, VRA Core, or CDWA. You might also need to translate records created with one of these standards into another standard. The process of doing this is called *mapping* or *crosswalking*. Although these two terms are often used interchangeably, mapping is often associated with determining how fields in one metadata schema are related to fields in another metadata schema, while crosswalking is running individual records through stylesheets to transform them into another metadata standard. Also, official tables showing relationships between metadata schemas, often maintained by an agency such as the Library of Congress, are referred to as *crosswalks*. In the Semantic Web, different approaches are possible due to the uncoupling of individual statements from an entire record. Maps showing the relationships between properties may become more useful than the current method of the best match between element definitions in different schemas (Dunsire et al., 2011, p. 6).

When creating local metadata fields, be sure to consider how these fields will map to common standards (Han et al., 2009, p. 235). At the very least, your local field definitions should map to Dublin Core fields. Use local value strings rather than local field naming conventions, and consider granularity when creating field names. For example, you may be tempted to create individual metadata fields for a journal citation in an electronic repository.

```
<Volume>23</Volume>
<Number>1</Number>
<Pages>14–20</Pages>
```

However, all of these fields will map to the Dublin Core Source field, producing the following:

```
<dc:source>23</dc:source>
<dc:source>1</dc:source>
<dc:source>14–20</dc:source>
```

Obviously, this is meaningless in an aggregated environment, and does not follow the best practices for sharing mentioned above. Instead of using local field naming conventions to identify the location, use local value strings, such as "Volume 23, no. 1, pages 14–20." When mapping to the Dublin Core Source field, this will appear as:

```
<dc:source>Volume 23, no. 1, pages 14-20</dc:source>
```

If the local fields are needed for internal processing, be sure that when mapping to Dublin Core the entire citation information is mapped to the source field. This follows our best practices and is meaningful to a user who finds the record in an aggregated database.

Additionally, you should determine which fields are local and only helpful in the local environment. For example, many institutions include administrative information in their records, such as the equipment used for the digitization project. While this may be useful locally, in an aggregated environment it isn't helpful, and creates additional noise in the results.

If you need to create more metadata fields outside the standard you're using for your records (many times this is done to record local information), you should take field names from other definitions. This will ensure that you're using a common element, and will make mapping to other schemas much easier. For example, if you want to record the nationality of an artist, but the Dublin Core standard you're following doesn't support this level of description, you can look instead to VRA Core 4.0 to see how they encode information about nationality.

If you're interested in more information about crosswalking, the Getty Institute maintains a Metadata Standards Crosswalk showing how elements in each standard relate to each other at *http://www.getty.edu/research/publications/electronic_publications/intrometadata/crosswalks.html*.

The Library of Congress maintains a MARC to DC crosswalk at *http://www.loc.gov/marc/marc2dc.html*, as well as DC to MARC crosswalk at *http://www.loc.gov/marc/dccross.html*.

XSLT

You may have previously heard the phrase "massaging the metadata." Metadata librarians often use this phrase when they transform metadata from one scheme to another scheme. Mapping is the intellectual activity of deciding how metadata elements in different schemas relate to each other, but the metadata needs to go through some transformations in order to make this happen. Most of the time, this is done by using XSLT. XSLT is a language for transforming XML documents into XHTML or other XML documents. This is useful for mapping between metadata schemas or displaying XML in a viewer friendly way. In addition to XSLT, a language called XPath is used to navigate through an XML document and point to a specific XML element or attribute.

XSLT is written in XML, and starts with <xsl:stylesheet> or <xsl:transform>. The XSLT namespace resides at *http://www.w3.org/1999/XSL/Transform*. There are lots of XSLT tutorials online, if you're interested in gaining more hands-on experience with XSLT. A good place to start is the w3schools.com XSLT Tutorial.

OAI-PMH

OAI-PMH was developed in 1999 as a low-barrier technology intended to help users find e-prints located in various repositories. OAI-PMH uses a *harvested* approach rather than the *federated* approach of metasearch. In a harvested approach, metadata is collected from selected databases and combined into one place, allowing users to search across metadata produced at different institutions in a single database and interface. Users of OAI-PMH are either data providers or service providers. Data providers create metadata and expose it to harvesters. Service providers return metadata records to the users and include links back to the original repository, or data provider. In this approach, content still resides in the original repository and service providers point back to it.

OAI-PMH is based on the HyperText Transfer Protocol (HTTP) and XML. This means that XML metadata records are transferred across the internet we're all familiar with, and the XML records can be viewed on a browser.

OAI-PMH requires that all metadata be exposed in Simple Dublin Core as a minimum, using the oai_dc XML schema. OAI-PMH also supports the exposure of other formats. Because of this, records for individual resources may be represented in several different metadata records and "languages," such as Dublin Core and VRA Core, but the identifiers all point back to the same resource.

OAI-PMH starts with a base URL of the repository. In an OAI request, the base URL is followed by a question mark and one of six verbs. The six OAI verbs are: Identify, ListSets, ListMetadataFormats, GetRecord, ListRecords, and ListIdentifiers. For example, the New Mexico Digital Collections (*http://econtent.unm.edu/*) has an OAI-PMH base URL of *http://econtent.unm.edu:81/cgi-bin/oai.exe*. If you enter this URL into a web browser, an XML record will be returned that says you have an "Illegal OAI verb." This is because you haven't specified a verb yet. One of the easiest requests is for identification information about the repository. You can request this by adding "?verb=Identify" to the end of the URL (*http://econtent.unm.edu:81/cgi-bin/oai.exe?verb=Identify*).

The first two verbs are used by themselves:

1. Identify. Provides a description of the archive. (Example: *http://econtent.unm.edu:81/cgi-bin/oai.exe?verb=Identify*)
2. ListMetadataFormats. Provides the types of metadata formats that records in the archive use. (Example: *http://econtent.unm.edu:81/cgi-bin/oai.exe?verb=ListMetadataFormats*)

The next verb may include a *ResumptionToken*. A ResumptionToken is used when many XML records are returned in a list, and the data provider's server may get overwhelmed by providing all of the records at the same time. Data providers can determine their own limit before providing a ResumptionToken. Generally 200–500 records are returned before a ResumptionToken is listed. ResumptionTokens are listed at the end of the results list and can be added to the original verb request. An example of a request with a resumption token is under #5 (ListRecords).

3. ListSets. Provides the structure of the archive/repository. In most repositories, like ContentDM and DSpace, sets correspond to collections, although this doesn't have to be the case. (Example: *http://econtent.unm.edu:81/cgi-bin/oai.exe?verb=ListSets*. All sets are returned in this example, and no ResumptionToken is needed.)

The next verb requires use of a *metadataPrefix*. As mentioned previously, OAI-PMH requires use of Dublin Core, but supports metadata in other formats. As long as each resource is described using Dublin Core, a data provider can also provide additional metadata records for the same resource in a different metadata language. For example, a resource could be described using both Dublin Core and VRA Core records. Because of this, when you request a record or records from a repository, you must specify which metadata type you'd like the record to be returned in.

In addition to the metadataPrefix, the following verb also requires use of an *OAI identifier*. The OAI identifier is not the resource identifier (e.g. dc:identifier). Instead, the OAI identifier identifies the XML record. You can find it in the header of the XML record.

4. GetRecord. Provides individual records (based on OAI identifier). Requires MetadataPrefix and Identifier. (Example: *http://econtent.unm.edu:81/cgi-bin/oai.exe?verb=GetRecord&identifier=oai:econtent.unm.edu:abqmuseum/0&metadataPrefix=oai_dc*)

In addition to metadataPrefix, and a possible ResumptionToken, the following two verbs also make use of *Set, From*, and *Until*.

Set specifies which set, returned from the ListSets command, you'd like the records to be from. The information is found in the <setSpec> field in the header of the XML record.

From and *Until* let you specify the date ranges of when the records were created. This is taken from the <datestamp> field in the XML header. Note that it is different from the dc:date field. The datestamp is recorded in YYYY-MM-DD format, and any level of granularity is accepted. If you would like all records created in 2009 you can use from=2009-01-01 and until=2009-12-31.

5. ListRecords. Returns complete records (number limited by data provider's repository, additional records returned by ResumptionToken). Requires MetadataPrefix. Optional Set, From and Until. May include ResumptionToken. (Examples: *http://econtent.unm.edu:81/cgi-bin/oai.exe?verb=ListRecords&metadataPrefix=oai_dc*; *http://econtent.unm.edu:81/cgi-bin/oai.exe?verb=ListRecords&resumptionToken=:::oai_dc:1000*; *http://econtent.unm.edu:81/cgi-bin/oai.exe?verb=ListRecords&metadataPrefix=oai_dc&from=2007-01-01&until=2009-12-31*.)
6. ListIdentifiers. Provides a list of OAI identifiers. Requires MetadataPrefix. Optional Set, From and Until. May include Resumption Token. (Example: *http://econtent.unm.edu:81/cgi-bin/oai.exe?verb=ListIdentifiers&metadataPrefix=oai_dc*.)

You can experiment with any open data provider. Many institutions open their ContentDM servers to harvesters. If you know of a ContentDM digital collection, you can include cgi-bin/oai.exe after the home URL to find the OAI-PMH base URL, in most cases. For example, New Mexico's Digital Collections (*http://econtent.unm.edu*) uses ContentDM, and the OAI-PMH base URL is *http://econtent.unm.edu:81/cgi-bin/oai.exe* (notice the addition of ":81" to the URL). From this URL, you can construct a request using the verbs above, for example, *http://econtent.unm.edu:81/cgi-bin/oai.exe?verb=Identify*. Some data providers do not share their metadata with harvesters, and their repository will not respond to an OAI request. Other data providers do not have a predictable OAI-PMH base URL, and you may need to email them and ask for it. More information about OAI-PMH can be found in *Using the Open Archives Initiative Protocol for Metadata Harvesting* (Cole and Foulonneau, 2007).

Exercises

- Query a data repository for its contact information. What is the administrator's email address?
- Query the repository for all records generated in the previous six months.
- How many sets does the repository use to organize its resources?

Although OAI-PMH was designed as a low-barrier method to sharing metadata records, many repositories choose not to share their records. Some of the reasons these repositories cite include a technical infrastructure that does not support OAI-PMH, metadata in an unshareable state, and the closed culture of various institutions.

Many institutions build their own digital object repositories without knowing how easy it is to share metadata through OAI-PMH. A wealth of information exists on the Open Archives website (*http://www.openarchives.org/pmh/*), and can be useful for explaining how to expose your institution's metadata through OAI-PMH.

Some institutions do not design their metadata elements with shareability in mind, and, as a result, do not feel ready to share their metadata with other institutions. Although this may be true of your metadata, it might be worth the effort of re-examining the metadata with shareability in mind, to determine what changes need to be made to bring it up to standard. Increased visibility of your metadata, and findability through other services, will bring more visitors to your site and make users more aware of your collections. You may even reach new users.

Additionally, libraries, archives, and museums all come from different backgrounds. Libraries generally share non-unique copies of books, and, as a result, cataloging has been seen as a community effort, especially when technology can help the process. However, archives and museums are used to dealing with unique resources, and cooperative cataloging isn't useful in this environment. The unique resources available through these institutions require individual cataloging, and metadata is institution specific. Now that resources are discoverable through the internet, there is no reason for any cultural heritage institution not to share metadata with potential users.

Conclusion

High quality metadata is important in the local environment because it helps your users find your resources. But the power of metadata can really be harnessed in the larger environment. Your collection may hold several thousand resources, but across the world, cultural heritage institutions hold billions of resources. Ensuring that your metadata is interoperable in this context will help researchers find information they need, and bring more attention to your collection.

In this book, we've given you a basic understanding of the theory and practice of metadata, examined Dublin Core, CDWA, VRA Core 4.0, and EAD, and presented a larger picture of how all of these metadata standards can fit together. Metadata creation may initially seem like an overwhelming task with different standards and vocabularies to choose from, but, as soon as you narrow your choices and see how each standard fits in your local environment, the correct path will become more obvious. Well-designed metadata can help your users find the information they need, understand the context of the resource and collection, and provide information about how to use the resource.

Where to go for more information

OAI for Beginners – the Open Archives Forum online tutorial *http://www.oaforum.org/tutorial/*

W3Schools.com. XSLT Tutorial *http://www.w3schools.com/xsl/default.asp*

Answer key

RDF exercise

01940162 has *date* 1923

01940162 has title *Cliff dwellings west of Santa Fe, NM*

01940162 has *type image*

01940162 has *description Postcard of cliff dwellings west of Santa Fe, NM*

Shareability exercise

First example:
First two description fields do not describe the image. Other description fields describe formats of digital files, and scanning specifications. This information, while helpful in a local environment, will create noise in an aggregated environment.

The format field describes the type of machine required to access the image. It should describe the format of the image (e.g. image/jpeg).

Second example:
Missing publisher information, relation information, source information, etc.

OAI-PMH exercise

1. Use the Identify verb. For example, *http://econtent.unm.edu:81/cgi-bin/oai.exe?verb=Identify*.
2. Use the ListRecords verb with metadataPrefix, from, and until. For example: *http://econtent.unm.edu:81/cgi-bin/oai.exe?verb=ListRecords&metadataPrefix=oai_dc&from=2012-01-01&until=2012-06-30*.
3. Use ListSets. For example: *http://econtent.unm.edu:81/cgi-bin/oai.exe?verb=ListSets*.

Appendix: XML examples

This appendix has XML records for exercises in Chapters 3 through 6. See Chapter 2 for an introduction to XML. Although you may never have to work directly in XML, you should be comfortable with interpreting an XML record, and understanding how the metadata is represented in XML. You may notice inconsistencies between records. All of these records are valid against the schemas, but individual institutions will need to create best practices for use within their institution.

Dublin Core (Chapter 3)

Exercise 3.1 Camel Rock, circa 1948

```
<metadata
  xmlns:xsi="http://www.w3.org/2001/XMLSchema-instance"
  xmlns:dc="http://purl.org/dc/elements/1.1/"
  xmlns:dcterms="http://purl.org/dc/terms/">
  <dc:title>Camel Rock, circa 1948</dc:title>
  <dc:subject>Camel Rock (N.M.)</dc:subject>
  <dc:publisher>New Mexico State University Library</
dc:publisher>
  <dc:type xsi:type="dcterms:DCMIType">Still Image</
dc:type>
  <dc:format>image/jpeg</dc:format>
  <dc:identifier>02231280</dc:identifier>
  <dc:language xsi:type="dcterms:ISO639-3">eng</dc:
language>
  <dcterms:isFormatOf>Ms02231280</dcterms:isFormatOf>
```

```
  <dcterms:isPartOf>Thomas K. Todsen Photograph
Collection, Ms0223</dcterms:isPartOf>
  <dc:rights>Copyright NMSU Board of Regents</dc:rights>
</metadata>
```

Exercise 3.2 Motorcycle Machine Gun Corp, Las Cruces

```
<metadata
  xmlns:xsi="http://www.w3.org/2001/XMLSchema-instance"
  xmlns:dc="http://purl.org/dc/elements/1.1/"
  xmlns:dcterms="http://purl.org/dc/terms/">
  <dc:title>Motorcycle Machine Gun Corp, Las Cruces</
dc:title>
  <dc:subject>Motorcycle Machine Gun Corp</dc:subject>
  <dc:subject>Machine guns</dc:subject>
  <dc:subject>Motorcycle sidecars</dc:subject>
  <dc:description>Handwritten caption on photograph reads,
"Motorcycle Machine Gun Corps, Las Cruces, 1913." Image
shows a number of motorcycles parked in a large, grassy
area. Digital image was created using Adobe Photoshop CS3
Macintosh, at 8 bits and 300 dpi.</dc:description>
  <dc:publisher>New Mexico State University Library</
dc:publisher>
  <dc:date xsi:type="dcterms:W3CDTF">1913</dc:date>
  <dcterms:created xsi:type="dcterms:W3CDTF">2009-02-
26</dcterms:created>
  <dc:type xsi:type="dcterms:DCMIType">Still Image</
dc:type>
  <dc:format>image/jpeg</dc:format>
  <dc:identifier>Ms00010258</dc:identifier>
  <dc:source>Ms0001, Box 4, Folder 3: black and white
photograph</dc:source>
  <dc:language xsi:type="dcterms:ISO639-3">eng</dc:
language>
  <dcterms:isFormatOf>Ms00010258</dcterms:isFormatOf>
  <dcterms:isPartOf>Branigan Memorial Library Photographs,
Ms0001</dcterms:isPartOf>
  <dc:rights>Copyright NMSU Board of Regents</dc:rights>
</metadata>
```

Exercise 3.3: Men bagging chili peppers

```
<metadata
  xmlns:xsi="http://www.w3.org/2001/XMLSchema-instance"
  xmlns:dc="http://purl.org/dc/elements/1.1/"
  xmlns:dcterms="http://purl.org/dc/terms/">
  <dc:title>Men bagging chile peppers</dc:title>
  <dc:subject xsi:type="dcterms:LCSH">Hot peppers</
dc:subject>
  <dc:subject xsi:type="dcterms:LCSH">Hot pepper
industry</dc:subject>
  <dc:description>Older database describes the image as,
"Seven men sacking chile peppers for commercial sale,"
and notes that the item is oversized. Digital image was
created using Adobe Photoshop CS5 Macintosh, at 24 bits
and 300 dpi.</dc:description>
  <dc:publisher>New Mexico State University Library</
dc:publisher>
  <dc:date>1920–1930</dc:date>
  <dcterms:created>2004-01-13</dcterms:created>
  <dc:type xsi:type="dcterms:DCMIType">Still Image</
dc:type>
  <dc:format>image/jpeg</dc:format>
  <dc:identifier>04500241</dc:identifier>
  <dc:source>ua04500241, mounted photographic print</
dc:source>
  <dcterms:isFormatOf>ua04500241</dcterms:isFormatOf>
  <dcterms:isPartOf>Fabian Garcia Papers, ua0450</
dcterms:isPartOf>
  <dc:rights>Copyright NMSU Board of Regents</dc:rights>
</metadata>
```

EAD (Chapter 4)

```
<ead>
  <eadheader audience="internal" langencoding="
iso639-2b">
    <eadid countrycode="us">New Mexico State University
Library</eadid>
```

```
    <filedesc>
      <titlestmt>
        <titleproper>Inventory of Photographs from the
New Mexico State University Library</titleproper>
        <author>Processed by A. Jackson, R. Lubas, and I.
Schneider</author>
      </titlestmt>
      <publicationstmt>
        <publisher>New Mexico State University Library,
Archives and Special Collections</publisher>
        <address><addressline>Archives and Special
Collections</addressline><addressline>4th Floor Branson
Library</addressline><addressline>New Mexico State
University</addressline><addressline>Las Cruces, New
Mexico</addressline></address>
        <date>2012</date>
      </publicationstmt>
    </filedesc>
    <profiledesc>
      <langusage>Finding aid is in <language>English</
language></langusage>
    </profiledesc>
    <revisiondesc>
    </revisiondesc>
  </eadheader>
  <frontmatter>
    <titlepage>
      <titleproper>Inventory of Photographs from the
New Mexico State University Library</titleproper>
      <num>Collection number: MSS 01</num>
      <publisher>New Mexico State University Library,
Archives and Special Collections</publisher>
      <date>Publication date: October 2012</date>
      <list>
        <head>Contact Information</head>
        <item>New Mexico State University Library</item>
        <item>Archives and Special Collections</item>
        <item>New Mexico State University</item>
        <item>Las Cruces, NM</item>
      </list>
      <list>
```

```
        <defitem>
          <label>Date processed:</label>
          <item>October 2012</item>
        </defitem>
      </list>
    </titlepage>
  </frontmatter>
  <archdesc level="collection">
    <did>
      <head>Collection Summary</head>
      <unittitle label="Title">Photographs from the
New Mexico State University Library, <unitdate
type="inclusive"
          >1913–1948</unitdate></unittitle>
      <unitid label="Collection Number">MSS 01</unitid>
      <origination label="Creator">
        <corpname>New Mexico State University Library
</corpname>
      </origination>
      <physdesc label="Size">
        <extent>1 folder (3 photographs)</extent>
      </physdesc>
      <repository label="Repository">
        <corpname>New Mexico State University. Archives and
Special Collections.</corpname>
      </repository>
      <physloc label="Shelf Location">For current
information on the location of these
        materials, please inquire at the access desk.
</physloc>
      <langmaterial label="Language">
        <language langcode="eng">English.</language>
      </langmaterial>
    </did>
    <scopecontent>
      <head>Scope and Content</head>
      <p>These three photographs are dated from 1913–1948,
and are included in The Metadata Manual: A Practical
Workbook for exercises and examples.</p>
    </scopecontent>
    <bioghist>
```

```
     <head>Institutional History</head>
     <p>These photographs, from the New Mexico State
University Library, are included in The Metadata Manual: A
Practical Workbook for exercise examples. </p>
   </bioghist>
   <descgrp type="admininfo">
     <head>Administrative Information</head>
     <accessrestrict>
       <head>Access Restrictions</head>
       <p>None</p>
     </accessrestrict>
     <userestrict>
       <head>Copy Restrictions</head>
       <p>User responsible for all
         copyright compliance.</p>
     </userestrict>
     <prefercite>
       <head>Preferred Citation</head>
       <p>New Mexico State University Library, Archives
and Special Collections, MSS 01</p>
     </prefercite>
   </descgrp>
   <controlaccess>
     <head>Access Terms</head>
     <subject source="lcsh">Motorcycle Machine Gun Corp</
subject>
     <subject source="lcsh"> Machine guns</subject>
     <subject source="lcsh">Motorcycle sidecars</subject>
     <subject source="lcsh"> Hot peppers</subject>
     <subject source="lcsh">Hot pepper industry</subject>
     <geogname>Camel Rock (N.M.)</geogname>
   </controlaccess>
   <dsc type="in-depth">
     <head>Contents List</head>
     <c01 level="item">
       <did>
         <container type="folder">1</container>
         <unittitle>3 photographs from various locations
in New Mexico.</unittitle>
       </did>
     </c01>
```

```
    </dsc>
  </archdesc>
</ead>
```

CDWA (Chapter 5)

Exercise 5.1: Scene at Santa Fe Station

```
<cdwa:cdwalite xmlns:cdwa="http://www.getty.edu/CDWA/
CDWALite"
  xmlns:xsi="http://www.w3.org/2001/XMLSchema-instance"
  xsi:schemaLocation="http://www.getty.edu/CDWA/CDWALite
http://www.getty.edu/CDWA/CDWALite/CDWALite-
xsd-public-v1-1.xsd">
  <cdwa:descriptiveMetadata>
    <cdwa:objectWorkTypeWrap>
      <cdwa:objectWorkType>digital image</cdwa:object
WorkType>
    </cdwa:objectWorkTypeWrap>
    <cdwa:titleWrap>
      <cdwa:titleSet>
        <cdwa:title>Scene at Santa Fe Station</cdwa:title>
      </cdwa:titleSet>
    </cdwa:titleWrap>
    <cdwa:displayCreator>unknown America</cdwa:display
Creator>
    <cdwa:indexingCreatorWrap>
      <cdwa:indexingCreatorSet>
        <cdwa:nameCreatorSet>
          <cdwa:nameCreator>unknown</cdwa:name
Creator>
        </cdwa:nameCreatorSet>
        <cdwa:nationalityCreator>American</cdwa:
nationalityCreator>
        <cdwa:roleCreator>artist</cdwa:roleCreator>
      </cdwa:indexingCreatorSet>
    </cdwa:indexingCreatorWrap>
    <cdwa:indexingMeasurementsWrap>
      <cdwa:indexingMeasurementsSet>
```

```
        <cdwa:formatMeasurements>JPEG</cdwa:format
Measurements>
      </cdwa:indexingMeasurementsSet>
    </cdwa:indexingMeasurementsWrap>
    <cdwa:displayMaterialsTech>digital imaging</cdwa:
displayMaterialsTech>
    <cdwa:indexingMaterialsTechWrap>
      <cdwa:indexingMaterialsTechSet>
        <cdwa:termMaterialsTech>digital imaging</cdwa:
termMaterialsTech>
      </cdwa:indexingMaterialsTechSet>
    </cdwa:indexingMaterialsTechWrap>
    <cdwa:displayCreationDate>unknown</cdwa:display
CreationDate>
    <cdwa:indexingDatesWrap>
      <cdwa:indexingDatesSet>
        <cdwa:dateQualifier>Date of original</cdwa:date
Qualifier>
        <cdwa:earliestDate>unknown</cdwa:earliest
Date>
        <cdwa:latestDate>1935-12</cdwa:latestDate>
      </cdwa:indexingDatesSet>
    </cdwa:indexingDatesWrap>
    <cdwa:locationWrap>
      <cdwa:locationSet>
        <cdwa:locationName>New Mexico State University
Library</cdwa:locationName>
      </cdwa:locationSet>
    </cdwa:locationWrap>
    <cdwa:indexingSubjectWrap>
      <cdwa:indexingSubjectSet>
        <cdwa:subjectTerm>Train stations</cdwa:subject
Term>
        <cdwa:subjectTerm>Santa Fe (N.M.)</cdwa:subject
Term>
      </cdwa:indexingSubjectSet>
    </cdwa:indexingSubjectWrap>
    <cdwa:descriptiveNoteWrap>
      <cdwa:descriptiveNoteSet>
        <cdwa:descriptiveNote>Image showing a scene from the
courtyard of the Santa Fe Station in Santa Fe, New Mexico.
```

```
Older database indicates the original item is a
photomechanical color print.</cdwa:descriptiveNote>
      </cdwa:descriptiveNoteSet>
    </cdwa:descriptiveNoteWrap>
    <cdwa:inscriptionsWrap>
      <cdwa:inscriptions>Handwritten captions along top
read "[Ms223, 466]" and "[RG88-168]." Printed caption on
the bottom reads, "Scene at Santa Fe Station."
</cdwa:inscriptions>
    </cdwa:inscriptionsWrap>
    <cdwa:relatedWorksWrap>
      <cdwa:relatedWorkSet>
        <cdwa:relatedWorkRelType>related to</cdwa:
relatedWorkRelType>
        <cdwa:labelRelatedWork>Ms02230466</cdwa:label
RelatedWork>
      </cdwa:relatedWorkSet>
      <cdwa:relatedWorkSet>
        <cdwa:relatedWorkRelType>part of</cdwa:related
WorkRelType>
        <cdwa:labelRelatedWork>Ms0223, Thomas K. Todsen
Photographs</cdwa:labelRelatedWork>
        <cdwa:locRelatedWork>New Mexico State University
Library</cdwa:locRelatedWork>
      </cdwa:relatedWorkSet>
    </cdwa:relatedWorksWrap>
  </cdwa:descriptiveMetadata>
  <cdwa:administrativeMetadata>
    <cdwa:rightsWork>Copyright NMSU Board of Regents</
cdwa:rightsWork>
  </cdwa:administrativeMetadata>
</cdwa:cdwalite>
```

Exercise 5.2: Automobile Road on La Bajada Hill

```
<cdwa:cdwalite xmlns:cdwa="http://www.getty.edu/CDWA/
CDWALite"
  xmlns:xsi="http://www.w3.org/2001/XMLSchema-
instance"
```

```
  xsi:schemaLocation="http://www.getty.edu/CDWA/CDWALite
http://www.getty.edu/CDWA/CDWALite/CDWALite-xsd-
public-v1-1.xsd">
  <cdwa:descriptiveMetadata>
    <cdwa:objectWorkTypeWrap>
      <cdwa:objectWorkType>digital image</cdwa:object
WorkType>
    </cdwa:objectWorkTypeWrap>
    <cdwa:titleWrap>
      <cdwa:titleSet>
        <cdwa:title>Automobile road on La Bajada Hill</
cdwa:title>
      </cdwa:titleSet>
    </cdwa:titleWrap>
    <cdwa:displayCreator>unknown American</cdwa:display
Creator>
    <cdwa:indexingCreatorWrap>
      <cdwa:indexingCreatorSet>
        <cdwa:nameCreatorSet>
          <cdwa:nameCreator>unknown American</cdwa:
nameCreator>
        </cdwa:nameCreatorSet>
        <cdwa:roleCreator>artist</cdwa:roleCreator>
      </cdwa:indexingCreatorSet>
    </cdwa:indexingCreatorWrap>
    <cdwa:indexingMeasurementsWrap>
      <cdwa:indexingMeasurementsSet>
        <cdwa:formatMeasurements>JPEG</cdwa:format
Measurements>
      </cdwa:indexingMeasurementsSet>
    </cdwa:indexingMeasurementsWrap>
    <cdwa:displayMaterialsTech>digital imaging</cdwa:
displayMaterialsTech>
    <cdwa:indexingMaterialsTechWrap>
      <cdwa:indexingMaterialsTechSet>
        <cdwa:termMaterialsTech>digital imaging</cdwa:
termMaterialsTech>
      </cdwa:indexingMaterialsTechSet>
    </cdwa:indexingMaterialsTechWrap>
    <cdwa:displayCreationDate>unknown</cdwa:
displayCreationDate>
```

```
    <cdwa:indexingDatesWrap>
      <cdwa:indexingDatesSet>
        <cdwa:dateQualifier>Date of original</cdwa:date
Qualifier>
        <cdwa:earliestDate>unknown</cdwa:earliest
Date>
        <cdwa:latestDate>1913-02</cdwa:latestDate>
      </cdwa:indexingDatesSet>
    </cdwa:indexingDatesWrap>
    <cdwa:locationWrap>
      <cdwa:locationSet>
        <cdwa:locationName>New Mexico State University
Library</cdwa:locationName>
      </cdwa:locationSet>
    </cdwa:locationWrap>
    <cdwa:indexingSubjectWrap>
      <cdwa:indexingSubjectSet>
        <cdwa:subjectTerm>La Bajada Hill (N.M)</cdwa:
subjectTerm>
        <cdwa:subjectTerm>United States Highway 66</
cdwa:subjectTerm>
      </cdwa:indexingSubjectSet>
    </cdwa:indexingSubjectWrap>
    <cdwa:descriptiveNoteWrap>
      <cdwa:descriptiveNoteSet>
        <cdwa:descriptiveNote>Image showing cars traveling
a hillside road with multiple switchbacks. Older database
indicates the original item is a tinted photomechanical
post card.</cdwa:descriptiveNote>
      </cdwa:descriptiveNoteSet>
    </cdwa:descriptiveNoteWrap>
    <cdwa:inscriptionsWrap>
      <cdwa:inscriptions>Printed caption on top left
reads, "Automobile Road on La Bajada Hill on 'Ocean to
Ocean Scenic Highway,' near Santa Fe, New Mexico."</
cdwa:inscriptions>
    </cdwa:inscriptionsWrap>
    <cdwa:relatedWorksWrap>
      <cdwa:relatedWorkSet>
        <cdwa:relatedWorkRelType>part of</cdwa:related
WorkRelType>
```

```
        <cdwa:labelRelatedWork>Ms0223, Thomas K. Todson
Photographs</cdwa:labelRelatedWork>
        <cdwa:locRelatedWork>New Mexico State University
Library</cdwa:locRelatedWork>
      </cdwa:relatedWorkSet>
    </cdwa:relatedWorksWrap>
  </cdwa:descriptiveMetadata>
  <cdwa:administrativeMetadata>
    <cdwa:rightsWork>Copyright NMSU Board of Regents
</cdwa:rightsWork>
  </cdwa:administrativeMetadata>
</cdwa:cdwalite>
```

Exercise 5.3: Danzante (matachin) group

```
<cdwa:cdwalite xmlns:cdwa="http://www.getty.edu/CDWA/
CDWALite"
  xmlns:xsi="http://www.w3.org/2001/XMLSchema-instance"
  xsi:schemaLocation="http://www.getty.edu/CDWA/CDWALite
http://www.getty.edu/CDWA/CDWALite/CDWALite-
xsd-public-v1-1.xsd">
  <cdwa:descriptiveMetadata>
    <cdwa:objectWorkTypeWrap>
      <cdwa:objectWorkType>digital image</cdwa:object
WorkType>
    </cdwa:objectWorkTypeWrap>
    <cdwa:titleWrap>
      <cdwa:titleSet>
        <cdwa:title>Danzante (matachin) group</cdwa:
title>
      </cdwa:titleSet>
    </cdwa:titleWrap>
    <cdwa:displayCreator>unknown</cdwa:display
Creator>
    <cdwa:indexingCreatorWrap>
      <cdwa:indexingCreatorSet>
        <cdwa:nameCreatorSet>
          <cdwa:nameCreator>unknown</cdwa:name
Creator>
        </cdwa:nameCreatorSet>
```

```
        <cdwa:roleCreator>photographer</cdwa:role
Creator>
      </cdwa:indexingCreatorSet>
    </cdwa:indexingCreatorWrap>
    <cdwa:indexingMeasurementsWrap>
      <cdwa:indexingMeasurementsSet>
        <cdwa:formatMeasurements>JPEG</cdwa:format
Measurements>
      </cdwa:indexingMeasurementsSet>
    </cdwa:indexingMeasurementsWrap>
    <cdwa:displayMaterialsTech>digital imaging</cdwa:
displayMaterialsTech>
    <cdwa:indexingMaterialsTechWrap>
      <cdwa:indexingMaterialsTechSet>
        <cdwa:termMaterialsTech>digital imaging</cdwa:
termMaterialsTech>
      </cdwa:indexingMaterialsTechSet>
    </cdwa:indexingMaterialsTechWrap>
    <cdwa:displayCreationDate>2009-02-19</cdwa:
displayCreationDate>
    <cdwa:indexingDatesWrap>
      <cdwa:indexingDatesSet>
        <cdwa:dateQualifier>Date of original</cdwa:date
Qualifier>
        <cdwa:earliestDate>1907-01-01</cdwa:earliest
Date>
        <cdwa:latestDate>1907-12-31</cdwa:latestDate>
      </cdwa:indexingDatesSet>
    </cdwa:indexingDatesWrap>
    <cdwa:locationWrap>
      <cdwa:locationSet>
        <cdwa:locationName>New Mexico State University
Library</cdwa:locationName>
      </cdwa:locationSet>
    </cdwa:locationWrap>
    <cdwa:indexingSubjectWrap>
      <cdwa:indexingSubjectSet>
        <cdwa:subjectTerm>Matachines (Dance)</cdwa:
subjectTerm>
      </cdwa:indexingSubjectSet>
    </cdwa:indexingSubjectWrap>
```

```
    <cdwa:descriptiveNoteWrap>
      <cdwa:descriptiveNoteSet>
        <cdwa:descriptiveNote>Description in older database
reads, "Danzante (matachin) group, man third from right is
Cenovio Avalos, second from right is Francisco Dominguez.
Las Cruces or Tortugas, New Mexico," and indicates that the
original is a glass negative. Image shows a group composed
of men in costume and young girls in white dresses.
Digitized using Adobe Photoshop CS3 Macintosh, at 8 bits,
300 dpi.</cdwa:descriptiveNote>
      </cdwa:descriptiveNoteSet>
    </cdwa:descriptiveNoteWrap>
    <cdwa:relatedWorksWrap>
      <cdwa:relatedWorkSet>
        <cdwa:relatedWorkRelType>related to</cdwa:
relatedWorkRelType>
        <cdwa:labelRelatedWork>Ms00040260</cdwa:
labelRelatedWork>
        <cdwa:locRelatedWork>New Mexico State University
Library, Archives and Special Collections Department, Rio
Grande Historical Collections</cdwa:locRelatedWork>
      </cdwa:relatedWorkSet>
      <cdwa:relatedWorkSet>
        <cdwa:relatedWorkRelType>part of</cdwa:related
WorkRelType>
        <cdwa:labelRelatedWork>Ms0004 Amador Family
Papers</cdwa:labelRelatedWork>
        <cdwa:locRelatedWork>New Mexico State University
Library, Archives and Special Collections Department, Rio
Grande Historical Collections</cdwa:locRelatedWork>
      </cdwa:relatedWorkSet>
      <cdwa:relatedWorkSet>
        <cdwa:relatedWorkRelType>part of larger context</
cdwa:relatedWorkRelType>
        <cdwa:labelRelatedWork>Rocky Mountain Online
Archives, Register of the Amador Family Papers, 1836–
1949, http://rmoa.unm.edu/docviewer.php?docId=nmlcu1
ms4.xml</cdwa:labelRelatedWork>
      </cdwa:relatedWorkSet>
    </cdwa:relatedWorksWrap>
  </cdwa:descriptiveMetadata>
```

```
  <cdwa:administrativeMetadata>
    <cdwa:rightsWork>Copyright NMSU Board of Regents</
cdwa:rightsWork>
  </cdwa:administrativeMetadata>
</cdwa:cdwalite>
```

VRA (Chapter 6)

Exercise 6.1: Booth of Casey-Ranch, Roswell Apple Show

```
<vra xmlns="http://www.vraweb.org/vracore4.htm"
  xmlns:xsi="http://www.w3.org/2001/XMLSchema-instance"
  xsi:schemaLocation="http://www.vraweb.org/vracore4.htm
http://www.vraweb.org/projects/vracore4/
vra-4.0-restricted.xsd">
  <work id="w_04500236" refid="Ms04500236">
    <agentSet>
      <display>unknown (American)</display>
      <agent>
        <culture>American</culture>
      </agent>
    </agentSet>
    <culturalContextSet>
      <culturalContext>American</culturalContext>
    </culturalContextSet>
    <dateSet>
      <display>1911-10</display>
      <date type="creation">
        <earliestDate>1911-10</earliestDate>
        <latestDate>1911-10</latestDate>
      </date>
    </dateSet>
    <descriptionSet>
      <description>Image of a decorative produce display
at the Roswell Apple Show. Display contains arranged
crates showcasing a number of different types of apples.
Identification signs among the crates read "Bellflower",
"Vandi Ver Pippin", "R.I. Greening", "Keiffer Pears",
"Apple-Commerce", "Gano", and "Blacktwig."</description>
```

```
    </descriptionSet>
    <inscriptionSet>
      <inscription>
        <position>Bottom right</position>
        <text>Winner of 5-Blue-Ribbons, 1 Second + Diploma,
Roswell Apple Show. Oct, 5, 6, 7, 1911, copyright 1912 by
L.W. Adams.</text>
      </inscription>
    </inscriptionSet>
    <locationSet>
      <location type="repository">
        <name type="corporate">New Mexico State University
Libraries (Las Cruces, New Mexico, United States)</name>
      </location>
      <location type="site">
        <name type="geographic">Roswell (N.M.)</name>
      </location>
    </locationSet>
    <materialSet>
      <material>Photographic prints</material>
    </materialSet>
    <relationSet>
      <relation type="depicts">Booth of Casey Ranch,
Roswell Apple show</relation>
    </relationSet>
    <rightsSet>
      <rights type="copyrighted">
        <text>Copyright NMSU Board of Regents, Please
send questions to archives@lib.nmsu.edu</text>
      </rights>
    </rightsSet>
    <subjectSet>
      <subject vocab="LCSH" refid="n 80150257">
        <term type="geographicPlace">Roswell (N.M.)</term>
      </subject>
      <subject>
        <term type="corporateName">Casey Ranch</term>
      </subject>
      <subject>
        <term type="otherName">Roswell Apple Show</term>
      </subject>
```

```
      <subject vocab="LCSH" refid="sh 85002317">
        <term type="descriptiveTopic">Agricultural
exhibitions</term>
      </subject>
      <subject vocab="LCSH" refid="sh 85047239">
        <term type="descriptiveTopic">Farm
produce</term>
      </subject>
    </subjectSet>
    <titleSet>
      <display>Booth Casey-Ranch, Roswell Apple Show </
display>
      <title type="descriptive" pref="true" xml:lang="
en">Booth Casey-Ranch, Roswell Apple Show </title>
    </titleSet>
    <worktypeSet>
      <worktype vocab="AAT" refid="300127104">
Photographic Prints</worktype>
    </worktypeSet>
  </work>
  <image id="i_04500236" refid="04500236">
    <dateSet>
      <display>2004-01-13</display>
      <date type="creation">
        <earliestDate>2004-01-13</earliestDate>
        <latestDate>2004-01-13</latestDate>
      </date>
    </dateSet>
    <descriptionSet>
      <description>Digitized at 24 bits and 200 dpi</
description>
    </descriptionSet>
    <relationSet>
      <relation type="imageOf" relids="w_04500236"></
relation>
    </relationSet>
    <techniqueSet>
      <display>digital imaging</display>
      <technique/>
    </techniqueSet>
    <titleSet>
```

```
      <title>Digitized image from black &amp; white
photograph</title>
    </titleSet>
    <worktypeSet>
      <display>digital image</display>
      <worktype/>
    </worktypeSet>
  </image>
</vra>
```

Exercise 6.2: Cliff dwellings west of Santa Fe, N.M.

```
<vra xmlns="http://www.vraweb.org/vracore4.htm"
  xmlns:xsi="http://www.w3.org/2001/XMLSchema-instance"
  xsi:schemaLocation="http://www.vraweb.org/vracore4.htm
http://www.vraweb.org/projects/vracore4/
vra-4.0-restricted.xsd">
  <work id="w_01940162" refid="Ms01940162">
    <agentSet>
      <display>unknown (American)</display>
      <agent>
        <culture>American</culture>
      </agent>
    </agentSet>
    <culturalContextSet>
      <culturalContext>American</culturalContext>
    </culturalContextSet>
    <dateSet>
      <display>1923</display>
      <date type="creation">
        <earliestDate>1923</earliestDate>
        <latestDate>1923</latestDate>
      </date>
    </dateSet>
    <descriptionSet>
      <description>Photographic print of cliff dwellings
west of Santa Fe, New Mexico.</description>
    </descriptionSet>
    <inscriptionSet>
      <inscription>
```

```
        <position>Bottom</position>
        <text type="caption">Cliff dwelling west of Santa
Fe, N.M., 1923</text>
      </inscription>
    </inscriptionSet>
    <locationSet>
      <location type="repository">
        <name type="corporate">New Mexico State University
Libraries (Las Cruces, New Mexico, United States)</name>
      </location>
      <location type="site">
        <name type="geographic">Santa Fe (N.M.)</name>
      </location>
    </locationSet>
    <relationSet>
      <relation type="partOf">Leslie K. Goforth Photograph
Collection, Ms 0194</relation>
    </relationSet>
    <rightsSet>
      <rights type="copyrighted">
        <text>Copyright NMSU Board of Regents, Please send
questions to archives@lib.nmsu.edu</text>
      </rights>
    </rightsSet>
    <subjectSet>
      <subject vocab="LCSH" refid="sh 85027024">
        <term>Cliff-dwellings</term>
      </subject>
      <subject vocab="LCSH" refid="n 79055800">
        <term type="geographicPlace">Santa Fe (N.M.)
</term>
      </subject>
    </subjectSet>
    <techniqueSet>
      <technique vocab="AAT" refid="300054225">
photography</technique>
    </techniqueSet>
    <titleSet>
      <title>Cliff dwellings west of Santa Fe., N.M.</
title>
    </titleSet>
```

```
    <worktypeSet>
      <worktype vocab="AAT" refid="300046300">
photographs</worktype>
    </worktypeSet>
  </work>
  <image id="i_01940162" refid="Ms01940162">
    <relationSet>
      <relation type="imageOf" relids="w_01940162"></
relation>
    </relationSet>
  </image>
</vra>
```

Exercise 6.3: La Fonda, the Harvey Hotel at Santa Fe, New Mexico

```
<vra xmlns="http://www.vraweb.org/vracore4.htm"
  xmlns:xsi="http://www.w3.org/2001/XMLSchema-instance"
  xsi:schemaLocation="http://www.vraweb.org/vracore4.htm
http://www.vraweb.org/projects/vracore4/
vra-4.0-restricted.xsd">
  <work>
    <agentSet>
      <display>Isaac Rapp (American architect, 1854-
1933)</display>
      <agent>
        <name vocab="ULAN" refid="500068773" type="
personal">Rapp, Isaac</name>
        <dates type="life">
          <earliestDate>1854</earliestDate>
          <latestDate>1933</latestDate>
        </dates>
        <culture>American</culture>
        <role>architect</role>
      </agent>
    </agentSet>
  <culturalContextSet>
      <culturalContext>American</culturalContext>
  </culturalContextSet>
```

```
    <dateSet>
      <date type="creation">
        <earliestDate>1922</earliestDate>
        <latestDate>1922</latestDate>
      </date>
    </dateSet>
    <descriptionSet>
      <description>The La Fonda Hotel is located on the
Plaza in Santa Fe, New Mexico, on what has been called the
oldest hotel corner in America.</description>
    </descriptionSet>
    <locationSet>
      <display>Santa Fe, New Mexico</display>
      <location type="site">
        <name type="geographic" vocab="LCSH" refid="n
79055800">Santa Fe (N.M.)</name>
      </location>
    </locationSet>
    <subjectSet>
      <subject vocab="LCSH" refid="nr2003034869">
        <term type="corporateName">La Fonda (Hotel: Santa
Fe, N.M)</term>
      </subject>
      <subject vocab="LCSH" refid="sh2008105800">
        <term>Hotels–United States</term>
      </subject>
    </subjectSet>
    <titleSet>
      <title>La Fonda Hotel</title>
    </titleSet>
    <worktypeSet>
      <worktype vocab="AAT" refid="300007166">hotels
(public accommodations)</worktype>
    </worktypeSet>
  </work>
  <work id="w_02230353" refid="Ms02230353">
    <agentSet>
      <display>Fred Geary (1894-1946)</display>
      <agent>
        <name>Geary, Fred</name>
        <dates type="life">
```

```
        <earliestDate>1894</earliestDate>
        <latestDate>1946</latestDate>
      </dates>
      <culture>American</culture>
      <role>painter</role>
    </agent>
  </agentSet>
  <culturalContextSet>
    <culturalContext>American</culturalContext>
  </culturalContextSet>
  <dateSet>
    <date>
      <earliestDate circa="true">1920</earliestDate>
      <latestDate circa="true">1940</latestDate>
    </date>
  </dateSet>
  <descriptionSet>
    <description>Photomechanical color postcard showing
a painting by Fred Geary of the La Fonda Hotel from a
nearby intersection.</description>
  </descriptionSet>
  <inscriptionSet>
    <inscription>
      <position>bottom</position>
      <text type="caption">H-3977 La Fonda, the Harvey
Hotel at Santa Fe, New Mexico. After painting by Fred
Geary.</text>
    </inscription>
  </inscriptionSet>
  <locationSet>
    <location type="repository">
      <name type="corporate">New Mexico State
University Libraries (Las Cruces, New Mexico, United
States)</name>
    </location>
  </locationSet>
  <relationSet>
    <relation type="partOf">Thomas K. Todsen Photograph
Collection</relation>
  </relationSet>
  <rightsSet>
```

```
      <rights type="copyrighted">
        <text>Copyright NMSU Board of Regents. Please send
questions to archives@lib.nmsu.edu</text>
      </rights>
    </rightsSet>
    <subjectSet>
      <subject vocab="LCSH" refid="nr2003034869">
        <term type="corporateName">La Fonda (Hotel: Santa
Fe, N.M)</term>
      </subject>
      <subject>
        <term>Harvey Hotels</term>
      </subject>
      <subject vocab="LCSH" refid="n 79055800">
        <term type="builtworkPlace">Santa Fe (N.M.)</term>
      </subject>
    </subjectSet>
    <techniqueSet>
      <technique vocab="AAT" refid="300041424">Photomechani
cal processes</technique>
    </techniqueSet>
    <titleSet>
      <title>La Fonda, the Harvey Hotel at Santa Fe
</title>
    </titleSet>
    <worktypeSet>
      <worktype vocab="AAT" refid="300033618">photomechani
cal prints</worktype>
    </worktypeSet>
  </work>
  <image id="i_02230353" refid="Ms02230353">
    <relationSet>
      <relation type="imageOf" refid="02230353"></relation>
    </relationSet>
    <techniqueSet>
      <display>digital imaging</display>
      <technique></technique>
    </techniqueSet>
    <titleSet>
      <title>Digitized image from photomechanical
postcard</title>
```

```
    </titleSet>
    <worktypeSet>
      <display>digital image</display>
      <worktype></worktype>
    </worktypeSet>
  </image>
</vra>
```

References

Works cited

Baca, M., Harpring, P., Lanzi, E., McRae, L. and Whiteside, A. B. (2006) *Cataloging Cultural Objects: A guide to describing cultural works and their images* (Chicago: ALA Editions).

Baca, M. (2007) CCO and CDWA Lite: "Complementary data content and data format standards for art and material culture information," *VRA Bulletin* 34(1): 69–75.

Beacom, M. (2007) 'Cataloging Cultural Objects (CCO), Resource Description and Access (RDA), and the future of metadata content," *VRA Bulletin* 34(1): 81–5.

Boughida, K. B. (2005) "CDWA Lite for Cataloguing Cultural Objects (CCO): A new XML schema for the cultural heritage community," in Association for History and Computing, Humanities, computers and cultural heritage. Proceedings of the XVI International Conference of the Association for History and Computing (AHC) 14–17 September 2005, 49–54 (Amsterdam: Royal Netherlands Academy of Arts and Sciences).

Coburn, E., Lanzi, E., O'Keefe, E., Stein, R. and Whiteside, A. (2010). "The Cataloging Cultural Objects experience: Codifying practice for the cultural heritage community," *IFLA Journal* 36(1): 16–29.

Cole, T. W. and Foulonneau, M. (2007) *Using the Open Archives Initiative Protocol for Metadata Harvesting* (Westport, CT: Libraries Unlimited).

Dublin Core Metadata Initiative (2011a) *User guide*. Retrieved August, 2012 from the DCMI Wiki: *http://wiki.dublincore.org/index.php/User_Guide*

Dublin Core Metadata Initiative (2011b) "Dumb down principle," in Dublin Core Metadata Initiative, *Glossary*. Retrieved August, 2012 from the DCMI Wiki: *http://wiki.dublincore.org/index.php/Glossary/Dumb-Down_Principle*

Dunsire, G., Hillmann, D., Phipps, J. and Coyle, K. (2011) "A Reconsideration of Mapping in a Semantic World," in Dublin Core Metadata Initiative, Proceedings of the International Conference on Dublin Core and Metadata Applications, 2011, 12–25. Retrieved October 4, 2012 from: *http://dcpapers.dublincore.org/index.php/pubs/article/view/3622*

Eklund, J. (2007) "Herding cats: CCO, XML, and the VRA Core," *VRA Bulletin* 34(1): 45–68.

Elings, M. W. (2007) "Metadata for all: Description standards and metadata sharing across cultural heritage communities," *VRA Bulletin* 34(1): 7–14.

Federal Geographic Data Committee (FGDC) (n.d.) *The business case for metadata*. Washington, DC: Federal Geographic Data Committee, Updated

July 2012. Retrieved June, 2012 from: *http://www.fgdc.gov/metadata/metadata-business-case*

Getty Institute (2009) Baca, M. and Harpring, P. (eds), *Categories for the Description of Works of Art* (Los Angeles, CA: Getty Trust). Retrieved August, 2012 from: *http://www.getty.edu/research/publications/electronic_publications/cdwa/introduction.html*

Han, M. J., Cho, C., Cole, T. W. and Jackson, A. S. (2009) "Metadata for Special Collections in CONTENTdm: How to Improve Interoperability of Unique Fields through OAI-PMH," *Journal of Library Metadata* 9(3): 213–38.

Harold, E. R. and Means, W. S. (2001) *XML in a nutshell: A desktop quick reference* (Sebastopol, CA: O'Reilly).

Harpring, P. (2007) "CCO overview and description," *VRA Bulletin* 34(1): 34–44.

Hillmann, D., Coyle, K., Phipps, J. and Dunsire, G. (2010) "RDA Vocabularies: Process, Outcome, Use," *D-lib Magazine* 16: 1–2. Retrieved September 25, 2012 from: *http://dlib.org/dlib/january10/hillmann/01hillmann.html*

International Federation of Library Associations (IFLA) (2009) *Functional Requirements for Bibliographic Records*. Retrieved June, 2012 from: *http://www.ifla.org/files/cataloguing/frbr/frbr_2008.pdf*

Jackson, A. S. (2008) "Review: Cataloging Cultural Objects: A guide to describing cultural works and their images," *Technical Services Quarterly* 25(1): 107–9.

Lagoze, C. (2001) "Keeping Dublin Core simple: Cross-domain discovery or resource description?" *D-Lib Magazine* 7(1). Retrieved August, 2012 from: *http://www.dlib.org/dlib/january01/lagoze/01lagoze.html*

Library of Congress (2006) *Development of the Encoded Archival Description DTD*. Retrieved July, 2012 from: *http://www.loc.gov/ead/eaddev.html*

Library of Congress (2012) *Encoded Archival Description, Version 2002*. Retrieved July, 2012 from: *http://www.loc.gov/ead/*

Ma, J. (2009) "Metadata in ARL Libraries: A survey of metadata practices," *Journal of Library Metadata* 9(1–2): 1–14.

Miller, S. J. (2011) *Metadata for Digital Collections* (New York, NY: Neal Schuman).

Morgan, E. L. (2008) *XML in libraries: A workshop*. Retrieved July, 2012 from: *http://infomotions.com/musings/xml-in-libraries/*

National Information Standards Organization (NISO) (2004) *Understanding metadata* (Bethesda, MD: NISO Press). Retrieved August, 2012 from: *http://arizona.openrepository.com/arizona/bitstream/10150/105486/1/niso.pdf*

Shreeves, S. L., Riley, J. and Milewicz, L. (2006) "Moving towards shareable metadata," *First Monday* 11(8). Retrieved September 25, 2012 from: *http://firstmonday.org/htbin/cgiwrap/bin/ojs/index.php/fm/article/view/1386/1304*

Visual Resources Association (n.d.) *VRA Core 3.0*. Retrieved February 5, 2013 from: *http://www.vraweb.org/projects/vracore3/index.html*

W3C (2003) *Extensible Markup Language (XML)*. Retrieved July, 2012 from: *http://www.w3.org/XML/*

W3Schools (2012) *XML elements*. Retrieved February 5, 2013 from: *http://www.w3schools.com/xml/xml_elements.asp*

Wayne, L. (2005) *Institutionalize metadata before it institutionalizes you* (Washington, DC: Federal Geographic Data Committee). Retrieved June,

2012 from: *http://www.fgdc.gov/metadata/documents/InstitutionalizeMeta_Nov2005.doc*

Weibel, S., Godby, J., Miller, E. and Daniel, R. (1995) *OCLC/NCSA Metadata Workshop report*. Retrieved August, 2012 from: *http://xml.coverpages.org/metadata.html*

Wendler, R. (2004) "The eye of the beholder: Challenges of image description and access at Harvard," in Hillmann, D. I. and Westbrooks, E. (eds), *Metadata in Practice*, 51–69 (Chicago: ALA Editions).

Zeng, M. L. and Qin, J. (2008) *Metadata* (New York: Neal-Schuman Publishers).

Works consulted

California Digital Library (2005) *OAC best practice guidelines for EAD*. Retrieved February 5, 2013 from: *http://www.cdlib.org/services/dsc/contribute/docs/oacbpgead_v2-0.pdf*

DCMI Usage Board (2012) *DCMI metadata terms (DCMI recommendation)*. Retrieved February 5, 2013 from: *http://dublincore.org/documents/dcmi-terms/#H3*

Dublin Core Metadata Initiative (2012) *User guide/creating metadata*. Retrieved February 5, 2013 from: *http://wiki.dublincore.org/index.php/User_Guide/Creating_Metadata*

Dublin Core Metadata Initiative (2012) "DCMI type vocabulary," in DCMI Usage Board (2012) *DCMI metadata terms (DCMI recommendation)*. Retrieved February 5, 2013 from: *http://dublincore.org/documents/dcmi-terms/#H7*

Encoded Archival Description Working Group of the Society of American Archivists and the Network Development and MARC Standards Office of the Library of Congress (2002) *Encoded Archival Description tag library: Version 2002*. Retrieved February 5, 2013 from: *http://www2.archivists.org/sites/all/files/EAD2002TL_5-03-V2.pdf*

Harold, E. R. and Means, W. S. (2001) *XML in a nutshell: A desktop quick reference* (Sebastopol, CA: O'Reilly).

J. Paul Getty Trust (2006) *CDWA Lite: Specification for an XML schema for contributing records via the OAI Harvesting Protocol*. Retrieved February 5, 2013 from: *http://getty.edu/research/publications/electronic_publications/cdwa/cdwalite.pdf*

Jackson, A. S., Han, M. J., Groetsch, K., Mustafoff, M. and Cole, T. W. (2008) "Dublin Core Metadata Harvested through OAI-PMH," *Journal of Library Metadata* 8(1): 5–18.

Library of Congress (2012) *EAD best practices at the Library of Congress* (Washington, DC: Library of Congress). Retrieved February 5, 2013 from: *http://www.loc.gov/rr/ead/lcp/*

RLG EAD Advisory Group (2002) *RLG best practice guidelines for Encoded Archival Description*. Retrieved February 5, 2013 from: *http://www.oclc.org/research/activities/past/rlg/ead/bpg.pdf*

Ruth, J. E. (1997) "Encoded Archival Description: A structural overview," *The American Archivist* 60(3): 310–29. Retrieved February 5, 2013 from: ***http://www.jstor.org/stable/40294440***

Shreeves, S. L., Knutson, E. M., Stvilia, B., Palmer, C. L., Twidale, M. B. et al. (2005) "Is 'Quality' Metadata 'Shareable' Metadata? The Implication of Local Metadata Practice on Federated Collections," in Thompson, H. A. (ed.), Currents and convergence: Navigating the rivers of change: Proceedings of the Twelfth National Conference of the Association of College and Research Libraries, April 7–10 2005, Minneapolis, MN, 223–37 (Chicago: Association of College and Research Libraries).

Visual Resources Association (n.d.a) *VRA Core 3.0*. Retrieved February 5, 2013 from: ***http://www.vraweb.org/projects/vracore3/index.html***

Visual Resources Association (n.d.b) *VRA Core 4.0*. Retrieved February 5, 2013 from: ***http://www.vraweb.org/projects/vracore4/***

Visual Resources Association (n.d.c) *VRA Core schemas and documentation*. Retrieved February 5, 2013 from: ***http://www.loc.gov/standards/vracore/schemas.html***

Visual Resources Association (2007) *VRA Core 4.0 element description*. Retrieved February 5, 2013 from: ***http://www.loc.gov/standards/vracore/VRA_Core4_Element_Description.pdf***

W3CSchools (2012) *XML elements*. Retrieved February 5, 2013 from: ***http://www.w3schools.com/xml/xml_elements.asp***

W3schools. (2012) *XSLT Tutorial*. Retrieved September 25, 2012 from: ***http://www.w3schools.com/xsl/default.asp***

Further reading

For RDA

Coyle, K. (2010) *Understanding the Semantic Web: Bibliographic data and metadata*. ALA Techsource.

Index

Lightning Source UK Ltd.
Milton Keynes UK
UKOW04f0448120914

238419UK00007B/69/P